D0983876

**Marcia Allentuck** teaches in the Department of English and Comparative Literature in The City College of the City University of New York. Her essays on eighteenth-century literature and the fine arts have appeared in many scholarly journals and she is completing books on Henry Fuseli and on the brothers Singer. She has also written on Yiddish literature for *Commentary*.

**Harry T. Moore** is Research Professor at Southern Illinois University. Among his recent books are *Twentieth-Century French Literature to World War II*, *Twentieth-Century French Literature since World War II*, and *Twentieth-Century German Literature*. He is coauthor of *D. H. Lawrence and His World*.

Isaac Bashevis Singer was born in Radzymin, Poland, in 1904. He grew up in Warsaw, where he was educated by his father, a rabbi, and at a rabbinical seminary. He began writing fiction while still in his teens. In 1926 he became a journalist, and worked for the Yiddish newspapers in Warsaw until 1935, when he came to the United States. Since coming to this country, he has worked for the *Jewish Daily Forward* and has translated many books into Yiddish from Hebrew, Polish, and German. A number of Singer's works have been translated into English, with several more scheduled to be translated. Isaac Bashevis Singer's novels which are available in English translations are *Satan in Goray*, *The Family Moskat*, *The Magician of Lublin*, *The Slave*, and *The Manor*. Also available are his autobiography, *In My Father's Court*, and several collections of short stories: *Gimpel the Fool*, *The Spinoza of Market Street*, *Short Friday*, and *Seance*.

*Crosscurrents*/MODERN CRITIQUES

Harry T. Moore, *General Editor*

2.50

# The Achievement of Isaac Bashevis Singer

EDITED BY

*Marcia Allentuck*

WITH A PREFACE BY

Harry T. Moore

SOUTHERN ILLINOIS UNIVERSITY PRESS
Carbondale and Edwardsville

FEFFER & SIMONS, INC.
London and Amsterdam

## Preface

In thinking over this Preface in advance and looking again through my collection of Isaac Bashevis Singer's books, I found myself quoted on the jacket of the first English-language edition of Short Friday and Other Stories (Farrar, Straus and Giroux, 1964). I'd forgotten this and can't trace the review quoted from, but will repeat that jacket excerpt from it because it says what I really feel about Singer:

> One of the really great novelists of today. This reviewer has no vested interested in Polish towns and stories set in them, but he admires depth and intensity in writing, and these qualities Isaac Bashevis Singer has in high degree. He writes in Yiddish, but so powerfully that the force of his work comes through in English translations.

In regard to Singer's being called one of our great novelists, this has become a commonplace. He continues to grow in stature. As for the remark about Polish towns (made before I had visited Singer's native Poland), I was stressing the difference between my own life-experience and his, yet indicating how much the power of his writing compels one's interest and sympathy. This is certainly the experience of most of us who read him in English: he takes us directly into his world and makes it ours, as the first-rate writer usually does. Seventeenth-century Goray and early twentieth-century Warsaw become part of our own experience.

As for the writing itself—what we usually call style —we discover immediately that it is one of the important characteristics of Singer. He originally wrote in Hebrew, but finally found his true mode of expression in Yiddish. Because he has lived in this country since 1935 (some of his stories are set here), he of course knows English well, but prefers to write his ambitious books in Yiddish and then work with his translators as they put the material into English. As Professor Allentuck notes in her Introduction that follows, Singer has been fortunate in his translators. There is Saul Bellow, for example, who translated that famous story, "Gimpel the Fool." The poet Elaine Gottlieb has also translated Singer, and so has her late husband, the novelist and editor Cecil Hemley. Perhaps because these writers, and others not mentioned here, have usually worked so closely with Singer—perhaps because of this, his original power comes through. And in this epoch of sloppy writing in our fiction, of what I have elsewhere called grocery-list prose, Singer's language is always stimulating, wonderfully matching the subject matter of his work.

That work is expertly discussed in the following essays, which have not previously appeared in print. Four introductory chapters deal with special aspects of Singer's work, including his place in the classical Yiddish tradition, the "duality and vision" found in his fiction, and his use of the grotesque. After that, seven essays investigate individual works. This is a well-planned book, and these essays are full of critical richness. The volume is a well-deserved and illuminating tribute to an author of Singer's significance.

Southern Illinois University   **HARRY T. MOORE**
March 21, 1969

## Acknowledgments

We wish to express our appreciation to Isaac Bashevis Singer for permission to quote from all his works, and to Harper and Row for the use of brief quotations from the children's story *Zlateh the Goat* (1966).

We also wish to thank the publishers Farrar, Straus and Giroux, Inc. for their permission to use short quotations from the following books: *The Family Moskat* © 1950, *Satan in Goray* © 1955, *Gimpel the Fool* © 1957, *The Spinoza of Market Street* © 1958, 1960, 1961, *The Magician of Lublin* © 1960, *Short Friday* © 1961, 1962, 1963, 1964, *In My Father's Court* © 1962, 1963, 1964, 1965, 1966, *The Slave* © 1962, *The Manor* © 1967, *Mazal and Schlimazel* © 1967, *The Seance* © 1964, 1965, 1966, 1967, 1968, all Copyright © by Isaac Bashevis Singer.

M. A.

## Notes on Contributors

MARCIA ALLENTUCK teaches in the Department of English and Comparative Literature in The City College of the City University of New York. Her essays on eighteenth-century literature and the fine arts have appeared in many scholarly journals and she is completing books on Henry Fuseli and on the brothers Singer. She has also written on Yiddish literature for *Commentary*.

WILLIAM H. GASS has written widely praised fiction (*Omensetter's Luck*; *In the Heart of the Heart of the Country*) and teaches Philosophy at Purdue University, and is a Guggenheim Fellow for 1969–70. He contributes essays and reviews on literary and philosophical subjects to numerous periodicals and now reviews fiction regularly for *The New York Review of Books*.

ELI KATZ teaches German and Yiddish at the University of California, Berkeley. A specialist in mediaeval Yiddish, he is also working on a long study of the distinguished modern Yiddish writer, David Bergelson.

MORRIS GOLDEN, a member of the Department of English at the University of Massachusetts, Amherst, is a Guggenheim Fellow for 1968–69. In addition to many shorter pieces on the eighteenth century, he has written books on William Cowper, Samuel Richardson, Thomas Gray, and Henry Fielding.

MAXIMILLIAN E. NOVAK, a former Guggenheim Fellow, teaches in the Department of English at the University of California, Los Angeles. He has written several books on Daniel Defoe and many articles on eighteenth-century fiction.

EDWIN GITTLEMAN, a member of the Department of English at Dartmouth College, has worked primarily on nineteenth-century American literature. His book on Jones Very was published by Columbia University Press under the terms of the Ansley Award and he is currently completing a book on Ralph Waldo Emerson.

MAX F. SCHULZ, Chairman of the Department of English at the University of Southern California, has written books and articles on Samuel Taylor Coleridge and the American Jewish novel. He is completing a book on Bruce Jay Friedman.

CYRENA N. PONDROM teaches Comparative Literature at the University of Wisconsin, and writes for *Wisconsin Studies in Contemporary Literature*.

FREDERICK R. KARL teaches in the Department of English and Comparative Literature in The City College of the City University of New York. He has written many books on the modern novel, including *The Contemporary English Novel, An Age of Fiction: The Nineteenth-Century British Novel* and *C. P. Snow*. He held a Guggenheim Fellowship in 1966–67 to work on his collected edition of the letters of Joseph Conrad.

MARY ELLMANN has published a number of reviews and articles in periodicals such as *Commentary* and *Encounter*. Her book, *Thinking About Women*, a social commentary on the novel, was published last year.

H. R. WOLF, who teaches English at the State University, Buffalo, has written on literature and psychology for such periodicals as *American Image* and *The Psychoanalytic Review*.

PAUL N. SIEGEL, Chairman of the Department of English at Long Island University, has published widely in the areas of Shakespeare and the English Renaissance, as well as in American literature. He has written two books on Shakespeare and edited a third.

# Contents

# Introduction

For at least a decade now, critical respect for the sustained intensity of Isaac Bashevis Singer's literary imagination and its fictive embodiments has grown virtually by geometric progression. Blakean in his precise, sensuous renderings of the literal and the visible, while "showing forth" the energies of the transcendental and the invisible, Singer negotiates swiftly and glitteringly, with deceptive and harrowing simplicity, among the moral climates of the divine, the human, and the demonic. Whether set in the East European Jewish *shtetls* now irretrievably lost through German genocide, or in declining side streets off New York's Central Park West—to name but a few of his expressive ambiences—his works levitate beyond the local facts of manners, rituals, and beliefs. With the consummate skill born of the authority and the power of his revelations, he arrests and ignites modern sensibilities: his name is now one to conjure with. Singer's thrust as a writer is rich but unprogrammatic. His enigmatic treatments of the tilted paradoxes and grotesqueries inherent in the conflicts between divine promise and experiential reality, redemption and history, religion and secularism, tradition and modernism, eroticism and self-discipline—such Singer-haunted dualities can be multiplied without end—speak to our human condition. Singer has learned to live by means of questions. The deeply perceived antitheses of which he writes he does not sentimentalize, justify, or attempt to resolve. The strength of their reverberations persists because of the intelligence of his vision and not because of its finalities. Unlike many of his modern readers, even disciples, Singer has assimilated and made the stuff of his fiction this painful, cardinal reality: that both the sacred and the profane can be merciless and absurd, however temporarily transmuted and salvaged by comedy and compassion, or leavened by exemplary "as if" impulses of regeneration, courage, and growth.

The essays in this collection were written specifically for it, and appear in print for the first time. Each contributor, a well-known writer in his or her own areas of specialization, was invited to examine, not to proclaim or protect, Singer's work. No central unifying mandate was inflicted by the editor: each person was invited to range at will through Singer's created universe and to embody responses to its qualities freely, as he or she was moved to do. Despite the resultant (and predictable) variousness, even the controversial qualities of some of the reactions and interpretations, all are linked by convictions of the depth and diversity of Singer's talent, of the essential relevance of his public and private lineaments. The discerning discussions are informed by the recognition that Singer, as man and as artist, is autonomous. To use Henry James's memorable description of a Lower East Side Jew in a rather ambivalent passage in *The American Scene*, Singer is "savingly possessed of everything that is in him," as echo of Singer's own assertion in the Introduction to his collected memoirs, *In My Father's Court*, that "only that which is individual can be just and true."

The organization of the essays is quite simple: four

pieces of a comprehensive cast concerned with general themes, motifs, techniques, connections, and continuities in Singer's novels and short stories lead into seven discussions in depth of specific works, arranged with one exception according to the original chronology of the appearances of Singer's works in English translations. The exception is the analysis of Singer's character, the more-than-outsider, more-than-insider Gimpel, that "attractive, God-annointed fool," as Norman Mailer unerringly dubs him. Saul Bellow's sensitive translation of Singer's Yiddish short story, *"Gimpel Tam,"* appeared in *Partisan Review* in 1953, perhaps even heralding Herzog, but certainly proclaiming Singer's arrival among readers of English as a master of that genre. Many believe that this work is still the jewel of Singer's crown. Certainly it has been anthologized and translated into other tongues besides English more than any of his other short works. I myself believe that the dissonances and working resolutions of most of Singer's major themes converge in this fragile, terrible and sanctified fable which, incidentally, is a pure example of his supple and pointed Yiddish prose style. The tale stands on its own and does not need to be validated by relating it to western analogues, but of all his works it shows most forcefully the play of his own original vision against the backdrop of an archetypal theme of western literature. Thus I have exercised editorial discretion by suspending chronology, just as Gimpel suspended skepticism—for a higher purpose. I have placed the analysis of it last, as a kind of apocalyptic omega for the collection.

I hope that this volume will afford pleasure and profit to at least two kinds of potential readers. I have first considered the general reader who has scant knowledge of the growth, content, and traditions of Yiddish literature but who, through sensitivity neither to modishness nor trendiness of cults but to the intelligent directions of the sensibilities and styles of modern (I do not say "contemporary" advisedly, wishing to avoid its pejorative ring) literary currents, now finds this literature and its most distinguished, if not its most traditionally characteristic living representative no longer remote from his interest. He is first discovering Singer's works in the English translations available only recently. For Singer's earliest novel, *Satan in Goray*, serialized in his native Poland's Yiddish periodical, *Globus*, in 1934, when Singer was thirty, was not translated into English until 1955, twenty years after Singer himself had settled permanently in America. *The Family Moskat*, while serialized in the American Yiddish daily, the *Forward*, 1945–48, was obtainable in an abridged English version in 1950, and only reissued in 1965. Three additional novels from his large body of Yiddish serializations in the *Forward* are available in English: *The Magician of Lublin* (1960); *The Slave* (1962); and *The Manor* (1967). The last named will be republished soon in amplified form together with its sequel, *The Estate*. Translations of other novels—*Shadows on the Hudson* and *A Ship to America*, are promised in the foreseeable future. Also published have been four collections of shorter fiction: *Gimpel the Fool and Other Stories* (1957); *The Spinoza of Market Street* (1961); *Short Friday* (1964); and *The Séance and Other Stories* (1968). Many uncollected stories, already translated into English, have recently been appearing in periodicals such as *Commentary* and *The New Yorker*, and fresh work in Yiddish appears steadily in the *Forward*, to which Singer has remained loyal (just as he has abided with his original publishers, Farrar, Straus and Cudahy, now Farrar, Straus and Giroux) even in these halcyon days of international fame and financial success. The autobiographical memoir, *In My Father's Court* (1966), and four books of children's stories (*The Fearsome Inn*; *Mazel and Schlimazel*; *When Shlemiel Went to Warsaw*; and *Zlateh the Goat*, published by Harper and Row by special arrangements with Singer's publishers) complete the list of book-length works in English translations. A few articles and reviews, many of them in the continental tradition of the *feuilleton*, have also appeared, but the bulk of Singer's nonfiction, written under several journalistic pseudonyms, remains untranslated. Projects of translation from Yiddish to English move slowly because of Singer's scrupulous collaborations with his translators—in all of whom he has been fortunate—and his ongoing quest for perfect expressiveness as he continually revises the Yiddish originals. (Consistently alive to the validity of erotic analogies to all areas of human effort, he has often in conversations with me likened the hunt for the perfect translator for a specific work to man's search for the perfect woman.) To be sure, he is concerned with the accuracy of the translations of his works into all tongues, but it is the language of his adopted country that has engaged him most.

For this the more specialized reader who may or may not have Yiddish must be grateful. Even if he first enjoyed Singer in the original, he has the added assurance that the English texts have Singer's fortifying approval. Singer's presiding at the translations of his works, and his developing of new subjects in his mid-sixties based on his American experiences are both enriching phenomena for the would-be appreciator and critic. Both of the classes of readers I have designated will be concerned ultimately not only with Singer's themes and fictive techniques in themselves, but also with their relationships to the concepts and strategies of other literatures. I believe that these essays can motivate such concerns. They appear at a moment when the study of Singer is not yet an "industry," when he comes to us undiluted by critics' *excessive* hunting after sources, parallels and other devices which may be meant to illuminate initially, but often end up muddying and obfuscating the original. Singer is still in the prime of his creative life; his work is not embalmed like a bee in amber but reaches us directly and vividly. Documentation in these essays has been kept to a minimum, so that their readers can better assimilate the workings of Singer's imagination and their effects upon an eclectic and discriminating group of writers. As more of his works are translated, others will want to turn to questions of chronological growth, stylistic influences, social, political, and economic factors—even to parapsychology and, in detail, to Hebrew and Yiddish backgrounds. But this group of essays will, I trust, serve equally well to give fresh and expanding dimensions both to the familiar and to the new by primarily confronting the texts themselves.

I am grateful for the prompt, gracious, and unconditional cooperation of the contributors, and of Isaac Bashevis Singer, Yankel Allentuck, Isaaca Allentuck, and the many friends with whom I discussed this book. I deeply regret that three unforgettable men who stimulated and supported my interest in Singer's works are no longer living: my father, Reverend Isaac Epstein, who would divert me when I was a child by reading aloud the prose pieces by "Bashevis" and "Warshofsky" from the *Forward* in a rare Scots-Yiddish accent that, according to Singer's doctrine of the Hidden Powers, perhaps presaged the international appeal that Singer was later to achieve; Cecil Hemley, my erstwhile colleague and editor of the

Noonday Press, then a subsidiary of Singer's present publishers, and the person most responsible for the introduction of Singer to English readers; and Professor Uriel Weinreich, incumbent of the Atran Chair at Columbia University, whose untimely death in 1967 at the age of forty deprived comparative linguistics and Yiddish literature of a brilliant, humane, and sympathetic scholar. To their memory this collection is devotedly dedicated.

MARCIA ALLENTUCK

The City College of the City University of New York
February, 1969

The Achievement of ISAAC BASHEVIS SINGER

# The Shut-In

WILLIAM H. GASS

I. B. Singer's work is remarkable for a number of reasons. Critics have called it "modern." It is not. Most of his stories take place in the past, certainly; but Gide composing *le Roi Candaule,* or Camus his *Caligula,* write in an unmistakably modern way. Singer's stories turn so remote a corner in the history of human consciousness, they may give the impression of coming from the future when they are really returning from a circumnavigation of infinity . . . and by the back way. He writes in Yiddish, but he thinks in Hebrew; or if you like, in awfully early Greek. The characters Singer creates (like the world he makes), whether he puts them down in Poland or New York, whether they live in the sixteenth century or presently, are as distant from us as the aborigines. It isn't their funny beards or costumes; it isn't because they live by law in a book that's dead as dumbbells, or engage in quaint inter-Jewish squabbles; it isn't because their lives are so compressed by custom, so driven on by superstition, that we simply feel our age superior in light and air at least; it isn't even because goose-footed devils are as real as geese there, or that from time to time evil steals from one or other body-pox its part as plague-in-chief. I have already called Singer a shut-in: this, again, not because he writes in a fossil language, risking, yet escaping, the fate of Eugène Marais; or because the world is as much a magical volume of words for him as it is for any glossing cabbalist (since he is clearly a scholar, studies up, arranges and collects); but only because of the primitive materiality of his approach; thus what Singer's shut inside of is a metaphysics—honored, ancient —a metaphysics of that Word which once worked its way up into World, a philosophy of acts and not intentions, of prayers and rites, not states of soul, a universe in which nothing's real but *things*. There's no soul silliness in the old Old Testament, and the pneumatic psyche of the early Greek was blood, breath, shadow, water, fire, air . . . each quite substantial. So was insanity substantial, uncommon lust or rage; even eloquence belonged to property and might be stolen like one's money or one's wife. Dreams were other countries, relations attributes, and numbers round, triangular, oblong, or square. Sin was a contaminating miasma. To level the waves the Greeks would have thrown Jonah overboard too. Beliefs were commanded actions, and one's history was often just a thread between the shears. Who knew what the gods might do?

The names of Descartes, Leibniz, or Maimonides may be mentioned, but they never function structurally. (Dr. Fischelson studies Spinoza as though the *Ethics* were the *Torah*.) Singer frequently chooses a subject which might be called "the coming of modern consciousness," but the form of his fiction denies it ever came. The most important fact about a novelist is the kind of creation he commands, for he's the true god there—brooding, in the beginning, above a blank and dismal page. His book's in this sense sacred. He must be taken at His Word. Construction counts. It forms the world in the work we see. In the better novels, construction counts for everything, since everything is construction, and there are no "details." It's not merely the words the author puts down, then, which matter, but their type or kind, and the characteristic patterns they form, the facts (in this way) they compromise, and the manner of knowing that is therefore implied. Nor must we be bamboozled by small mimes or minor traits or little tics into supposing that our author's "modern." (There are few cozy asides to the reader, for example, no loud labels of value, or manifestos of artistic intention.) Robbe-Grillet's pathetic "scientific" recital of acts and objects reveals an almost total subjectivity. It's not the waves but the power which moves them we must measure. It is, however, true, that like Flaubert, Singer hides the arm which holds his hand. This is because, in this writer's world, everything is possible. It matters very little what is true. If something's not true now, it once was, or it will be; if it didn't happen here, it happened somewhere else. Look about. What is important is not what we may believe, but the way we choose to believe it—our fidelity, our heat. Men are moved by falsehoods just as fiercely as by truths. (This is the position, by the way, of Gimpel the fool.) Then too, times change. Opinions change. One view is nearly as bad as another . . . or as good. Evaluation—fevered praise or blame—how does it serve us? Our philosophies are partial, partisan; that is, they're human, and they will pass away. Only God, through every change, remains, though he stays hidden from us, dwells beyond us (just as Singer does), behind the blinding rays of heaven, out of sight. A sobering thought for the critic, bending over one of Singer's books, patiently construing.

The whole of Singer's fiction possesses this magnificent ontological equality (fables, fantasies, and fairy tales are therefore never out of place); it has exactly the material solidity it claims for everything, since everything is open, and in space. The sensational, the extreme and extraordinary, the violent, saintly, severe and the cruel, the divine, the human, the diabolical: all are mastered by his method, placed in a line on the same plane; ritual acts and uncontrollable savagery, marriage and murder, prayers and pogroms; for they are all acts, acts like tangible objects resting in the world. After all, the flower and the phallus both exist, so do stones in a wall, or passions in a person. This gives Singer an important freedom. If, on the one hand, facts are everything, on the other, everything can be factual. No mind and body problem here, no links to be forged between precept and object, or bridges to be built between nature and the unnatural, thought, dream, and thing. Whatever is, is matter in ritual motion. An intense sense of reality in the reader is the initial advantage. No one quite believes in any inner spirit but his own.

We have no acquaintance with another consciousness. Shut in, all we can *perceive* is a world of objects; all we can *feel* is ourselves. Pain in the person beside us is a cry and a grimace, a message sent from the inside, or so we read it, connecting our former hurts to this present crying, attributing our subjectivity to the friend we have injured, or the cat we've kicked. If we meet ourselves as strangers, "one hand asks the other by the pulse," as Donne avers, "and our eye asks our urine, how we do." But what of indemonstrable agonies, silent debates, terrors and angers repressed for a secret reason, at enormous spiritual expense: those internal stresses hidden from the eye like weakening steel in faltering bridges? Furthermore, one weeping can disguise a thousand griefs, each different. The tears do not distinguish. They rise in joy as well as sorrow. Emotion, by behavior, is only indicated, never uniquely differentiated. Acts have particularity, too, but only part of their nature is internally determined; the feelings exercise a limited control over their manifestations, for the world makes its demands as well; it imposes on the aims of actions all kinds of means and conditions; it requires material expression be given to the soul. When there seems to be a match, when the inner state receives complete expression, each pang in one represented by an appropriate ping in the other, as with an over-subtle actor, we find the gestures hard to read, the feeling difficult to define, for it's precisely *not* our own; from behavior so subjectively determined there's no path back unless we are prepared to imitate it, and to imitate it in the same external situation, in order to discover *what it does to us.* This world, so full, is that way empty; we therefore fill it with our feeling. However strange the acts, the age, the characters have no other souls than those the readers give them. Identification, on such grounds, is inevitable and easy.

We accompany a character as he leaves his house to enter a street. Hoofs ring on the cobbles, carts creak, vendors cry their wares. In Singer these sounds are never sounds *in* anyone. They are objects which we come upon impersonally; they are therefore as much ours as the character we are following. Water puddles, shadows gather, snow falls: these details are not selected in deference to a consciousness. Thoughts are given words, devils materialize psychology, or we read journals, letters, and diaries which do. Decay within, like the portrait of Dorian Gray, manifests itself conveniently in drooping eyes and sallowness, wrinkles, weight, complexion, posture, loss of hair. The ritual bath is neglected; a man fouls his mouth with less than purely kosher food, or buys new shoes and shaves his beard. Singer empties out the mind the way small boys turn out their pockets.

Here's the Warden, undertaken by Trollope:

> Mr. Harding is a small man, now verging on sixty years,
> but bearing few of the signs of age; his hair is rather
> grizzled, though not grey; his eye is very mild, but clear
> and bright, though the double glasses which are held
> swinging from his hand, unless when fixed upon his
> nose, show that time has told upon his sight; his hands
> are delicately white, and both hands and feet are small;
> he always wears a black frock coat, black knee-breeches,
> and black gaiters, and somewhat scandalises some of
> his more hyperclerical brethren by a black neck-hand-
> kerchief.

Notice how vague and diffident this description is.
Mr. Harding is *verging* on sixty years; his hair is *rather*
grizzled; he *somewhat* scandalizes *some* of his hyperclerical brethren. Despite their purposiveness, "black"
and "small" are repeated wearily. Almost nothing gets
said that isn't nervously retracted: "though" and
"but" are frequent. Trollope composes in precisely
similar breaths; "and" (that empty conjunction)
often serves him; "is" and "are" (the simplest and
most passive of connectives) everywhere prevail; and
the whole paragraph, in consequence, is slow. Slack
writing and amphibolous construction reinforce these
impressions in an undesirable way. Trollope characteristically works with externals, yet we can ask why this
passage lacks any vigorous externality.

Normally we see things swiftly, in a single act of
vision; we see grizzled Mr. Harding, we don't see
Harding, then his hair, and finally that same hair's
grizzled ratherness. Nor do we see a somewhat, unless
there's fog. On camera, hands aren't delicately white,
then small; they're small, white, delicate—at once.
*Noticing*, however, is another matter. We may notice,
first, the whiteness of the hands, and then in a moment also realize they're small; but noticing is a
subjective act, and requires the selective operations of

a mind. Mr. Harding is given his properties very sedately indeed, as though in thought, not observation. Really, the Warden isn't here, standing like a Christmas tree about to be hung with baubles. He's off in Barchester somewhere, doubtless, fulfilling his moral resolves. Presently, he is being *remembered*. We are not permitted to infer, either, that age has affected Mr. Harding's sight, we are told. We're also informed of something we might not have inferred: that his black neck-handkerchief has scandalized some of his brethren. This fact carries, in addition, the implication that the scandalized are hyperclerical. Obviously, the mind which Mr. Harding's dimly filtering through is Trollope's.

Now let Singer introduce Rabbi Benish:

Rabbi Benish was in his sixties, but his skin was still smooth, he had lost none of his white hair, and his teeth had not fallen out. When he crossed the threshold of the prayer house for the first time after many years—tall, big-boned, with a full, round, curly beard, his satin coat reaching to the ground, the sable hat pulled down over his neck—all those sitting there rose and pronounced the blessing in thanks to Him who revives the dead. For there had been reports that Rabbi Benish had perished in Lublin during the massacres on the eve of the Festival of Tabernacles in the year 1655. The fringes of the vest that Rabbi Benish wore between his shirt and coat tumbled around his ankles. He wore short white trousers, white stockings, and half-shoes. Rabbi Benish grasped between his index finger and thumb the thick eyebrow that hung over his right eye, lifted it the better to see, cast a glance at the darkened, peeling walls of the prayer house and its empty book chests, and loudly declared: "Enough! . . . It is the wall of our blessed God that we begin anew."

The Rabbi is soon in motion, and the passive verbs of linking are soon replaced with far more active ones, or they're eliminated in favor of direct qualification.

The Rabbi is busy: he crosses a threshold, he grasps, he lifts, he glances, he declares. His qualities also behave; they act or suffer action. His satin coat reaches, his hat's pulled down, the fringes of his vest tumble, even his eyebrows hang. His unmoving teeth and hair are said *not* to have fallen out. The scene is clear, animated, and nowhere darkened by the presence of mind.

Now for something else. Gradgrind has just informed us that what he wants is facts.

> The scene was a plain, bare, monotonous vault of a schoolroom, and the speaker's square forefinger emphasized his observations by underscoring every sentence with a line on the schoolmaster's sleeve. The emphasis was helped by the speaker's square wall of a forehead, which had his eyebrows for its base, while his eyes found commodious cellarage in two dark caves, overshadowed by the wall. The emphasis was helped by the speaker's mouth, which was wide, thin, and hard set. The emphasis was helped by the speaker's voice, which was inflexible, dry, and dictatorial. The emphasis was helped by the speaker's hair, which bristled on the skirts of his bald head, a plantation of firs to keep the wind from its shining surface, all covered with knobs, like the crust of a plum pie, as if the head had scarcely warehouse-room for the hard facts stored inside. The speaker's obstinate carriage, square coat, square legs, square shoulders—nay, his very neckcloth, trained to take him by the throat with an unaccommodating grasp, like a stubborn fact, as it was—all helped the emphasis.

Trollope's description has no shape; Singer's hasn't either. On his Dickens has imposed a rhetorical scheme which, conforming so perfectly to its content, has reshaped the "facts" (so hard for Gradgrind, so soft for Dickens) to give them feeling. Gradgrind takes his qualities from the air; sound itself has greatly helped to create him, especially the hissing *s*, and this has fastened him firmly in his medium—language—where he belongs. Metaphors play over Gradgrind like psychedelic lights. In short, where Singer has seen and Trollope remembered, Dickens has imagined; for it is the imagination which has made this masterful paragraph.

When Dickens' creatures speak, subjectivity flows as from a tap into the world: personal, poetic, unique; their talk is testimony, and a pure quality of soul. For Singer, speech is an act like tugging at one's beard. Announcement, it's something solely to be heard. "Gold, gold, gold," cries a seller of oranges. "Brothers, we are lost. Let us blaspheme God," says a horse dealer. "What is there to forgive? You have been a good and faithful wife," declares Gimpel the fool. The characters think, of course, but their thought is only reported to us; we don't see the process; we are handed careful sums. They lust; they fear; they wonder: all of which means that in very specified ways, they behave.

In a world where everything has a proper name and address in objective space, one might suppose a radical particularity was possible—not only possible, but necessary. Not quite. First of all, by simple mortals, such a world cannot be *seen*. We can only pretend it's there. We can only pretend to perceive like machines. Our observations do particularize, but they do so because we bring to them ourselves, our minds, our personal concerns. A God who has complete detachment might be able to do it. Gods, then—or machines. Yet language is a scarcely kettled stew of universals and universal connectives. The unique is not very easily rendered in its terms. And faithful to his method, Singer does not particularize, he *names*; the names form lists: lists of properties, of acts and objects.

> [An imp is hiding in a boudoir mirror] . . . my little charmer suspected nothing. She stroked her left breast, and then her right. She looked at her belly, examined her thighs, scrutinized her toes. Would she read her book? trim her nails? comb her hair?

It's these collections which are unique, not the things in them.

> [The imp wonders.] Should I seduce a rabbi's daughter? deprive a bridegroom of his manhood? plug up the synagogue chimney? turn the Sabbath wine into vinegar? give an elflock to a virgin? enter a ram's horn on Rosh Hashana? make a cantor hoarse?

Our sense of the uniqueness of any act or object described depends entirely on our sense of the uniqueness of the sentences comprising the description—i.e., their form. They cannot be merely unique in the story, they must be unique *in the language*. To say that someone—Ginger—went in and out of her house as though in a dream, does not particularize her action very much. To say that Ginger's house went in and out of *her*, does, and not only because such things don't happen very often. Coats regularly reach, but how often has a neckcloth been trained to take it wearer by the throat? Dickens has made Gradgrind real, in this sense, within a page. Another writer may need an outlined life, a book. But we shall still feel strangely far from him in that case, because his *distinct* presence has never, at any point, been felt. Singer's fiction is weak in this respect, and necessarily so, for his world does not permit the easy exercise of the relevant techniques: he cannot interiorize, he dare not distort or pattern too much (the public world remains anonymous), he leans heavily on impersonal, though significant, rituals, on items equally objective for everyone, and so he must use striking lists, rely on imps and devils of all kinds. We've seen many beards, but not so many cloven hoofs. Indeed, the moment the minions of Satan stir, the style rises with new heat to meet them.

You simply can't have everything. One method may deprive you of another. Joyce could never accomplish, though he uses up a city of details, Singer's fine solidity. James' characters are singularly vaporous, remarkable balloons whose skins are weightless and invisible.

Many of Singer's short stories are told in the first person. We know that the speaker is Jewish, but the voice is customarily noncommital, the voice of the chronicler, the voice of tradition, a chorus for the community. It allows itself from time to time a conventional sentiment, a little awe or wonder, worried warding-off. ("God forbid it should happen to any of us.") Only the demons are permitted a personality. They are always up to mischief, of course, and consequently they never see with the machine's divine neutrality. They are selfish, partial, and they tell us more plainly than anyone else how they feel. They are, in fact, entirely human. Subjectivity, perhaps, is the devil's true property. The last demon, in the story of that name, has a character distinctly his own, and Dickens might have made him. Almost. An important exception is Gimpel, God's fool. He speaks with an imp's cheery tone though he's not as wise. Always, imps *know*. He is devoted to his wife although she's whorish and cheats on him continually. For her he steals "macaroons, raisins, almonds, cakes." For us, he makes lists to prove his feelings:

> I loved the child madly, and he loved me to. As soon as he saw me he'd wave his little hands and want me to pick him up, and when he was colicky I was the only

one who could pacify him. I bought him a little bone
teething ring and a little gilded cap.

Gimpel does not differ a bit from the demon in this
need to establish behavioral proof: "I eat dust. I sleep
on a feather duster. I keep on reading gibberish."

Gimpel is God's fool because he still believes in
devils, dreams, and fairies. He can be tempted by one
to put a stream of his pee in the bread dough, but he
can be persuaded by another to bury what he's baked.
The rabbi whom the last demon fails to lure toward
sin does not wrestle with his conscience and then win;
he asks instead to see his tempter's feet. The coming
world is one where demons will not ply their trade
because the people there, having taken evil *in*, can sin
very well without them. "Satan has cooked up a new
dish of kasha." It's called enlightenment:

> The Jews have now developed writers. Yiddish ones.
> Hebrew ones, and they have taken over our trade. We
> grow hoarse talking to every adolescent, but they print
> their kitsch by the thousands and distribute it to Jews
> everywhere. They know all our tricks—mockery, piety.
> They have a hundred reasons why a rat must be kosher.
> All that they want to do is to redeem the world.

In the role of Messiah. In a world without God all is
fallen; there is no one—nothing—to seduce. No, subjectivity is not the devil's bailiwick, after all. And in a
brilliant and bitter passage, put in the mouth of the
final demon, Singer tells us why he prefers to remain
shut in the old ways like leaves closed between the
covers of a holy book:

> There are no more Jews, no more demons. The women
> don't pour out water any longer on the night of the
> winter solstice. They don't avoid giving things in even
> numbers. They no longer knock at dawn at the ante-
> chamber of the synagogue. They don't warn us before

emptying the slops. . . . The *Book of Creation* has been returned to the Creator. Gentiles wash themselves in the ritual bath. . . . There is no longer an Angel of Good nor an Angel of Evil. No more sins, no more temptations! The generation is already guilty seven times over, but Messiah does not come. To whom should he come? Messiah did not come for the Jews, so the Jews went to Messiah. There is no further need for demons. . . . I am the last, a refugee. I can go anywhere I please, but where should a demon like me go? To the murderers?

This demon lives at last only on a Yiddish book. He swallows the letters. The book itself is written in the manner of the moderns. "The moral of the book is: neither judge nor judgment." But the letters are still old-fashioned—some nourishment in them. And when the demon has sucked the substance from them, what then? will that be the end of him? will he die of uselessness and hunger, driven from his function the way the motored carriage drove the horse? He seems to think so, but we who've read his author know his outlook better. There's a new life waiting for him in these novels and these stories. However, he will have to make some slight adjustments. He will have to consent to live forever in a fiction. As for the rest of us, we readers, fallen Jew or faithless gentile: well, Isaac Bashevis Singer can be rabbi, if he wishes, for us all.

# Isaac Bashevis Singer and the Classical Yiddish Tradition

ELI KATZ

Isaac Bashevis Singer may well be the most widely read Yiddish author of all time. Yet the popularity of his works in translation is not parallelled in the original among readers of Yiddish. While most of Singer's works appeared first in the Yiddish press (the novels serialized in the manner generally characteristic of Yiddish literature since the nineteenth century), only a few can be bought in the original language. Lest this be attributed solely to the general indisputable decline in the audience for Yiddish writing, it may be pointed out that a recent catalogue which lists three titles by the prolific Singer offers no fewer than nine by Sholem Asch and seven by Singer's older brother Israel Joshua. It is in fact disconcerting to discover with what vehemence many intelligent and experienced Yiddish readers reject the works of Singer, branding them not only as "worthless," but as "pornographic" and even "degenerate." Evident in these evaluations, to be sure, is the anxiety of many Jews to conceal from alien eyes the unflattering aspects of East European Jewish life which Singer so frequently depicts. Today, moreover, this concern represents more than simply the traditional resolve to avoid exposing to anti-Semites Jewish *shtetl* life at its most vulnerable. It reflects as well the urgent and pious desire to protect from misinterpretation the vanished East European culture of which Yiddish literature is the product; a culture which, because of its catastrophic demise, is understandably surrounded with an elegiac aura.

Study of Yiddish literature, however, reveals that the classical Yiddish literary tradition itself is not predominantly one of prettification; that the sores and boils which afflicted East European Jewish life were plainly evident to the older writers and were unabashedly treated in their literary works. The observation that Isaac Bashevis Singer frequently presents Jews in "a bad light" is certainly accurate. But the same accusation could be made against I. L. Peretz, Sholem Asch, I. J. Singer, certainly Mendele Moykher Sforim, and even Sholem Aleichem. Nevertheless, however vaguely they perceive this, Singer does in fact represent a significant deviation from the tradition of Yiddish literature which most Yiddish readers accept and into which they expect modern Yiddish works to fit. The nature of this deviation is the concern of this essay.

In lamenting his enforced exile from Germany and his consequent loss of contact with the German public, Thomas Mann once described his books as the product of a reciprocal educational bond between nation and author, depending on shared assumptions which the author himself had helped to create. Such a description can to my knowledge nowhere more accurately be applied than to the works of the older generation of Yiddish writers. Mendele Moykher Sforim, Sholem Aleichem, and I. L. Peretz, the triad of "classical" Yiddish writers, display considerable and significant differences from one another with respect to theme, style, and literary attitude. But they were all in the first instance social writers. That is to say, they viewed their writing directly in the context of the audience for whom they wrote. Mendele describes the inner struggle which preceded his decision to brave ridicule by writing in the despised Yiddish tongue, instead of in Hebrew as previously. The struggle was resolved when he asked himself, "For whom am I working?" and the answer came in this form: "Let come what will; I will take pity on the Yiddish language, that outcast daughter. It is time to do something for the people." Sholem Aleichem refers to himself repeatedly as a *folksshrayber*, a writer of (for) the people, while one of Peretz's little known criticisms of Sholem Aleichem rests on the view that the latter "doesn't do things, doesn't call on people to do things —he laughs. And he makes us laugh."

This does not mean that classical Yiddish literature was necessarily programmatic. Mendele's work is openly tendentious, at first frankly preaching the message of enlightenment, a message whose inadequacy to the problem was progressively illuminated, even to the author himself, by the very fidelity and clarity with which Mendele depicted the Jewish life of his era. Neither Peretz nor Sholem Aleichem promotes a particular program in his writing, yet their works, with all of the patent differences between them, share certain characteristics which are also to be found in those of Mendele. Central to the similarity is the view that the *shtetl* life of nineteenth-century East European Jewry needed to be changed drastically, and the conviction that reform and progress were not only essential, but also possible. Mendele is unsparing in his castigation of Jewish civic leaders for their greed, ignorance, and complacency. Peretz writes scathingly of "dead towns" and Sholem Aleichem "begs the reader not to be offended that he speaks such harsh words to his Kasrilevke people. I am, you understand, my dear friends, myself a Kasrilevker." Common to all three writers, and of greater importance than the element of social criticism which is evident in these examples, is the assumption that the writer's function included the obligation to reproach, admonish, cajole, and encourage his readers. And this assumption was shared by the readers who valued "their" writers partly in proportion to their efficacy as teachers.

Nevertheless, with the exception of Mendele, the prevailing tone of classical Yiddish literature is not didactic. And even in the case of Mendele the author speaks as a member of the community from *within* the community to the membership as a whole, and thus feels free to criticize and attack without reservation its weaknesses and evils. It is the sense of community which is pervasive in the older Yiddish literary tradition. This has hardly escaped notice. However the frequent translation of this sense into the vague sensation of "warmth" which has come to be associated with Yiddish literature, and particularly with the works of Sholem Aleichem, rests upon the mistaken conclusion that the authors were describing a community actually achieved, rather than voicing their fervent aspirations toward community. All of the classicists in their different ways were concerned with the vast discrepancies between the community which ought to have been fostered by the precepts and practices which are virtually built into the traditional Jewish ethic—and what was the actual state of affairs. While the victimization of the *shtetl* Jews by the Czarist government is clearly portrayed, as well as their pauperization by economic forces beyond their control, the greatest indignation is reserved for those among the Jews who prey on other Jews or who are indifferent to their sufferings. Nor are such individuals portrayed as isolated exceptions. There is sufficient evidence to suggest that the older writers viewed social injustice within the Jewish *shtetl* as a prevailing rather than an exceptional evil. Despite this, they are never tempted to question the validity of the notion of Jewish community. With all the sympathy that they demonstrate toward the most downtrodden among the Jews, and their anger at the Jewish oppressors, they rarely approach class consciousness.

Without doubt there existed within the *shtetl* alongside of the social divisions and inequities, genuinely cohesive factors and even genuine feelings of community solidarity which crossed class lines. The concept of Jewish religion being the privilege of a chosen people whose distinctiveness was continually emphasized by their residence among an alien majority, made religious belief and practice virtually conterminous with internal solidarity. The very notion of the *knesses yisroel* was part of the sacred component of Jewish life. Not only did the many ritual practices and traditionally prescribed attitudes contribute to social cohesion within the *shtetl*, but no less importantly, the existence of the East European Jewish community as an enclave within a generally hostile environment. While the very rich could escape most of the disabilities of Jewishness in the pale, in the typical *shtetl* rich and poor shared at the very least the fear of pogroms. In spite of considerable ugly historical evidence of factions enlisting the aid of the government to defeat or suppress their rivals within the Jewish community, community solidarity was, at least in theory, viewed as necessary to protection and even survival, especially in times of increased pressures from without. For the classical Yiddish writers, therefore, and for much although by no means all of their readership, the integrity of the *shtetl* community was an axiomatic norm representing an ideal type, in spite of the serious deviations from it in practice.

It is not clear to what extent the classicists actually believed that their visions of Jewish community would be achieved. There is nevertheless implicit in traditional Yiddish literature the rationalist conviction that improvement was possible, that social controls could be imposed, and that the forces of cohesion could be made to prevail. These forces were regarded as fundamental, no matter how weak they had become, while the shocking conditions which the writers angrily exposed, even if predominant, were viewed as symptoms and consequences of the aberrant breakdown of social order. The founders were not only rationalists, but also, whatever their personal religious convictions, essentially secular writers. Their central literary concentration was upon "the Jewish question" and this meant for them, without exception, the question of the Jew in the modern world. None of them conceived of a Jewish solution in any sort of withdrawal from the world. As secular writers, to be sure, they reflected the concerns of only a segment of the Yiddish speaking population. Chassidim, for example, did not read Yiddish literature on principle for worldly literature was to them at worst *treyf* and at best trivial. Other segments of the population, particularly some varieties of Zionists, rejected Yiddish literature not for its secular orientation but for its use of the despised Yiddish *"zhargón"* as a literary vehicle. Nevertheless, a broad range of readers coming largely from the working and middle classes was secured. And the equally fervent commitment of the founders to communal integrity and to social justice made it possible for readers at every point of a spectrum ranging from class-conscious workers to comfortable *petit-commercants* to find in traditional Yiddish literature their cultural sustenance and an echo of their own *shtetl* experiences.

The *shtetl* of Isaac Bashevis Singer is at once both reminiscent of and strangely different from that of the Yiddish classicists. It has often been remarked that the body of traditional Yiddish literature offers so clear and detailed a picture of *shtetl* culture that it can serve virtually as a source of ethnographic data. To the insider, the reader who himself emerged from it, it is instantly recognizable. The outsider, on the other hand, requires elaborate explanations, or at least a glossary, to orient himself in the environment. Singer's *shtetl* presents largely the same landmarks. Yet it is unacknowledged by most remaining *shtetl* emigrants, while readers from "outside" appear to find their way about easily. Neither the motivations of Singer's characters nor their destinies are dependent on the specific cultural content of *shtetl* existence. His primary concern is with the perpetual struggle between good and evil for the soul of man; a struggle which goes on constantly, and primarily on a plane of human existence which has little to do with the rational. The physical as well as the cultural environment are important only as a viewing device through which this immanent struggle becomes manifest in dimensions which are temporally and spatially definable. The *shtetl* of the classicists is primarily comprehensible in terms of the social community which it represents or aspires to become. The *shtetl* of Singer is not a community at all. It is a society in disarray. Singer's *shtetl* is the *locus in nuce* of the *anomie* which he sees as endemic to the condition of the world.

In *The Family Moskat, The Slave,* and *Satan in Goray* the absence of stable social relations and effective social controls is literal and is historically conditioned. With some exceptions such a situation is implicit in most of Singer's work. This vision, however, is not primarily a comment on society. Singer is not in the first instance concerned with the pernicious effect of the dissolution of social bonds, although this is surely part of his theme in *Satan in Goray*. Rather, it permits the author virtually to ignore any distracting social context and allows him to present the actions and motivations of his people in a "pure," almost abstract light, unencumbered by the complications which would be entailed in placing them in a culturally delimited network of social relations. The *shtetl* which, incidentally, Singer does not describe in very great detail, thus serves him as a kind of stylized exotic backdrop before which pious Jews and demons can play out their roles with equal appropriateness. The fact that humans and devils appear equally real in Singer's *shtetl* suggests that his towns of Goray and Bilgoray, Frampol and Zamość, all of which can be located historically and geographically, are more products of the imagination than the invented Tuneyadevke and Glupsk of Mendele, or Sholem Aleichem's Kasrilevke and Kozodeyevke.

Singer's modernism as a Yiddish author consists in the fact that his concern is not primarily with the "Jewish question" but rather with the human condition; and moreover that those aspects of humanity which are to him most fascinating are the nonrational. His style is vividly realistic and this makes even more striking the impression, objectionable to many traditional Yiddish readers, that to the author a succubus and a *yeshiva bokher* are equally real. Traditional Yiddish literature did not exclude the occult. Faithful recorders that they were, the founders described many elements of folk belief in their works: blessings, curses, spirits, charms to ward off the evil eye, and the like. But these were always identified as superstition, as symptoms of backwardness, and were treated with ridicule or condescension. Mendele viewed them with the scornful laughter of the enlightened "modernist"; Sholem Aleichem with the indulgent amusement of a grandchild enjoying his grandmother's archaic antics. Peretz deliberately employed folk beliefs as literary devices and thus spared them his scorn. But, as can be seen in his Chassidic tales, he employed them for consciously rationalistic purposes, concerned with their metaphoric possibilities rather than with their significance to the nonrational component of human existence. The intensely traditionalist Chassidic milieu from which Singer came saw no sharp separation between the natural and the supernatural, nor, for that matter, between the religious and the magical. Singer's Chassidic *shtetl* (and we may stretch the term here to include the Warsaw of his childhood) is central to his writing not as a matrix for social relations but as an arsenal of characters, motifs, legends, and incidents, all having equal claim to reality as material for his writing. In Singer's literary *shtetl*, however, one distinction that was crucial to the Chassidic view appears to grow dim—the distinction between the sacred and the profane. If, as Emile Durkheim maintained, that which is sacred in any society stands in part for the society itself in the collective representations of its members, then the encroachment of the profane in Singer's *shtetl* becomes a metaphor for the asocial environment in which his stories occur.

Much has been made in the Yiddish criticism of Singer's writing of his alleged pornography. The accusation requires no refutation but its relevance to the acceptance of Singer's work by Yiddish readers is not without interest. Themes such as rape, prostitution, adultery, and sexual aberration are not new to Yiddish literature, going back as far as Sholem Aleichem

("The Man from Buenos Aires," "A Daughter's Grave"), and recurring frequently, for example, in the works of Sholem Asch and David Bergelson, both of whom are unhesitatingly admitted to the Yiddish canon. New in Singer is his attention to sexuality of both men and women as a serious motivating force in human conduct, and, of course, his fashionably frank description of sexual behavior, as well as other orders of physiological function. It might be noted that most of Singer's stories appeared first in the *Jewish Daily Forward*. This has made it easy for some critics to accuse him of exploiting sensationalism to please the "lower" tastes of *Forward* readers—a charge which has been leveled in general against the *Forward* since the days of Abraham Cahan. The readers of Yiddish *belles lettres* are an old-fashioned group, although no more so than their years entitle them to be. Moreover, they are for the most part readers who cultivated an interest in literature without the assistance of formal education, either through their individual efforts or in groups related to trade-unions, political organizations, or other voluntary associations interested in culture. To many of them, as is not uncommon with cultural *nouveaux arrivés*, culture is inseparable from gentility and the Yiddish genteel tradition rejects the sexual and physiological frankness in Singer's works as gratuitous vulgarity, which critics tend to explain in commercial terms.

Much more important with regard to his reception, however, is the fact that Singer, writing in Yiddish, does not write primarily as a Jewish writer in the sense in which Yiddish readers view the term. The destruction of the Yiddish speaking heartland and of its population in the early 1940's truncated the development of the Yiddish literary tradition at the point which it had reached in 1939. It also turned the attention of the Yiddish reader even further back, to fix for all time as typical of the vanished East European Jewish culture an idealized earlier *shtetl* which had in any case by that time ceased to exist. Since the 1940's Yiddish literature has to a considerable extent been concerned with the memorialization of this lost world of East European Jewry. For a number of individual writers, survivors of ghettos, death camps, and partisan groups, their writing is a personal act of piety. This is seen as the appropriate concern of Yiddish literature by large numbers of readers who themselves betray an acute awareness that they too are last survivors of a culture catastrophically destroyed, although on the explicit level many will deny the finality of such a judgment. Singer, who in *Satan in Goray* had already indicated the direction in which he was to proceed, continued along the path of modernism as part of the development of world literature in the forties, fifties, and sixties. His treatment of the human existential problem appears to Yiddish readers incomprehensibly aloof from the real, historical existential crisis which they experienced in their own lifetime. Whatever historic or sentimental bonds Singer the man and the Jew shares with the Yiddish reading public, the gulf between his literary premises and their expectations is vast. The assumptions shared by the classical Yiddish writers and their readers gave great moral relevance to their works within the Jewish community. The fact that Singer, using the same props, as it were, communicates primarily with a public to whom the *shtetl* is essentially alien, suggests to these readers that his work is somehow spurious.

The readers of classical Yiddish literature were conditioned to find in their reading indications of a rational world of progress, hope, and brotherly assistance, and the unmistakable assurance of the authors' adherence to these values. Singer describes instead an irrational, asocial universe where, as often as not, as one writer has said, the devil has the last word. Unable to reconcile his *shtetl* with "their own" *shtetl* as portrayed, for example, by Sholem Aleichem, it is perhaps not surprising that many Yiddish readers should express bewilderment as to which side Singer is really on.

# Dr. Fischelson's Miracle
## Duality and Vision in Singer's Fiction

MORRIS GOLDEN

The critical consensus on Singer, to which his *Commentary* interview (November, 1963), seems to lend his agreement, understands him as often a dualist, generally a visionary, and always an ironist—an odd lot of feet in one bed, as his Chelmer sages might observe. But the oddity does not have to be chaos; the feet in the story, after all, belong to sisters. Perhaps the ingredients of the mixture can be sorted out, and their family relationship defined, if we can isolate them in one story as well as in the work at large. One bed which is typically provided with such members is "The Spinoza of Market Street," where the vision is resolution of duality in miracle, and where dualism and miracle are examined ironically.

Like other prolific writers of fiction, Singer tends to shape human relationships according to recurrent patterns, and frequently in his writings these lead to either of two antithetical culminations: a vision of chaos, as in *Satan in Goray* or *The Family Moskat* or "The Destruction of Kreshev," or a vision of order and faith, as in "Short Friday" or "The Spinoza of Market Street." Not all of his fictions fit one or the other pattern, nor are these mutually exclusive, as witness *The Magician of Lublin* or *The Slave* or such haunting masterpieces as "The Shadow of a Crib" or

"A Wedding in Brownsville." But on the whole his fictive world shows contrasting elements either painfully separated by the consequences of routine selfishness or fused into unity through such miracles of faith as humble willingness to endure, mutual respect, or love. The miracle is the primal Jewish miracle, the coming of the Messiah, who is to reveal universal order, God's rule, despite the apparent dominance of impassioned chaos.

Very often Singer's narrative is concerned with the relations of two people, most likely a man and a woman matched (or mismatched) in marriage; as in the *Zohar* and other cabbalistic writing, a wedding is his preferred symbol of fusion of divergences, of ritual affirmation of faith in the order of the world and the community. In "The Spinoza of Market Street" the poles are so far apart that no valid resolution—at least no modern resolution, to apply Irving Howe's comment on Singer's art (*Commentary*, October, 1960; *Encounter*, March, 1966)—can fail to suggest irony. An elderly student of philosophy, a former yeshiva prodigy now alienated from orthodoxy by a passion for Spinoza, lies poor, ill, alone in a garret high above a Jewish slum in Warsaw, where he is nursed by his neighbor, the homely, mannish, illiterate marketwoman Dobbe. When she spontaneously shows her eagerness to marry and he ruefully agrees, a miracle of mutual compassion occurs, a miracle that is ratified by his startling virility on their wedding night. At least temporarily, they are both made whole by their awareness of each other as human beings. But the story resonates with implications of wider issues, as indeed the pattern, whether in part or fully developed, resonates through Singer's writings.

Since "The Old Man" (1933), major elements of the "Spinoza" story appear, though treated in different ways and going in different directions. In "The Old Man," the ninety-year-old hero, a symbol of Jewish endurance, makes his way from Warsaw to his *shtetl* in war time, is married to a deaf-mute spinster (who would otherwise be doomed to withering isolation), and miraculously fathers a child, whom he names Isaac. Though in many stories the tenuous balance of irony is replaced by less ambiguous failures to unite or failures after apparent union (e.g., "The Shadow of a Crib," "Big and Little," "Alone," "Taibels and Her Demon"), a very recent work suggests the persistence of the hopeful pattern for Singer: "The Letter Writer" (in the January 13, 1968, *New Yorker*) is startlingly like "Spinoza," except that the middle-aged hero, perhaps a student of *Herzog*, reaches out through letters to establish contact with others. When his job ends and he falls ill, the gentile Mrs. Beechman appears to nurse him, sent by a message from her dead grandmother, and together they officiate at a miracle of mutual concern; but with suitably minimizing irony, the miracle is ratified by a mouse. Even the title story of Singer's recent book for children, "Zlateh the Goat," follows an outline recognizably like that of "Spinoza." A boy, reluctantly leading the family goat to town for slaughter, is lost with her in a sudden and miraculously great snow storm; in a providential haystack, the boy keeps a channel in the snow cleared for breathing, and the goat provides milk for sustenance, so that through mutual help and developing love they survive three days in a hostile environment. Reduced here to a parable, and stripped of the ironic hedge demanded by adult experience, the essential issues are the same: archetypal male intellect and female warmth form a mystic and complete union.

Possibly because it is the most notable recurrent

festival—exclusive of holidays—in the *shtetl*, and certainly because it is the most evident human attempt to unite opposites in man with the divine, the wedding is the pervasive Singer symbol for an attempted miracle. Indeed, all his weddings invoke the supernatural—though too often through human corruption they become symbols for the specious cover of evil, the operation of the human demonic, of black magic, as in *Satan in Goray* or "The Destruction of Kreshev" or the recent "Two Corpses Go Dancing" in *The Séance*. The wedding provides for Singer the supreme device for testing alternatives, the "as if" in life by which, like other copious story tellers, he has long been fascinated. Between Meshulam's third marriage, a sign of his dotage which opens *The Family Moskat*, and Hadassah's death to release Asa Heshel at the end, the coupling of pair after pair is chronicled and duly tested for intensity of fusion. *The Manor* begins with the wedding of Calman Jacoby's oldest daughter, comes to a climax in his own disastrous remarriage, and ends with his spiritual resurgence when he is reunited with the life of the synagogue. In the stories, the consequences of matches and mismatches show the mystery—the human significance—as far more important than the expectations of surrounding society. The famous "Gimpel the Fool," for example, centers in a marriage between a fool and a slut which is an ironic joke to the beholders (adult mankind), but it turns out a miracle of affection at least for him, and it ends with his subjective vision of her saintliness. In "The Man Who Came Back," on the other hand, the wife's love is almost as unstinted as Gimpel's, but it merely recalls to life a weakling who dwindles into a criminal. In "Blood," marriage between an old man and a young woman leads to great trouble, as does a mismatch of size in "Big and Little"; but the apparently greater disorder of "Esther Kreindel the Second," where the man is quite old and the girl very young, is in fact both right and miraculous. "A Wedding in Brownsville" seems an impossible hodgepodge of the living and dead, and yet is an exalted miracle; but the walking dead who marry in "Two Corpses Go Dancing" fall straight down to hell, since they are selfish puppets, not aspirants with faith.

The evident symbolic importance of union or failure to unite suggests a related symbolic element in Singer's art, his concern for archetypes, almost for allegories. As various critics have shown, Singer everywhere works with the archetypal Jewish experience, with representative Jews, and eventually with Man. As his miracles are affirmations of order in the world and the mind, his horrors are all versions of the Nazi horror, which becomes in turn symbolic of the ultimate consequences of ungoverned human nature. His larger figures are aspects of the Jew in response to permanently recurring experiences; and when, for example, Gombiner in "The Letter Writer" sees himself as Boas to Mrs. Beechman's Ruth, Singer is playing in one way with the possible union of Jew and gentile with which he had worked in other ways in the novels, particularly *The Slave* and *The Magician of Lublin*.

All of Singer's novels, whether realistic or symbolic in technique, are more or less direct examinations of such fundamental patterns. In *The Family Moskat* as in *The Manor* the figures stand all too evidently for aspects of the Polish Jew—and further, as Asa Heshel is aware, of disintegrating Modern Man—in the period between the Enlightenment and the catastrophe. As critics have suggested, *The Slave*, with a hero named Jacob who is serving among the heathen and takes a bride from his captors, is even more patently allegorical than the earlier *Satan in Goray*. Like that first novel, it is set immediately after the Chmelnicki horror, a type of catastrophe visited on Jews specifically but also on all that is civilized in man, all that is to carry the Law, and brought on by both the luxurious selfishness of the civilized and the naked brutality of the savage. Wanda's brother Antek, a representative bitter and violent peasant, hates Jacob, as Magda's brother Bolek in *The Magician* hates her Jewish lover: bringing to the fore the customary warning in Yiddish soap opera and folk tradition against chasing *shicksas* whose brothers have knives and no moral restraints, the greater warning against arousing the bestiality of the unenlightened toward the people chosen to carry the Law, the civilized warning against the savage's crude violence, and finally the warning to the mind and spirit of danger from the prideful passions. Sarah adores Jacob and has awaited him since childhood: the fertile passions of the people yearn toward the Messiah, and its union with him is sanctified by a miracle.

In *The Magician of Lublin*, which Singer described in his *Commentary* interview as "a morality tale," the hero, with an extraordinary mind and talent, is an ironic version of Jacob the slave-Messiah, of modern and indeed eternal Jewry: the artist-scientist (a magician in his two roles), with some of the alienation of Dr. Fischelson the affirming philosopher and Asa Heshel Bannet and Ezriel Babad the doubting philosophers, the sensual fantasies of Sabbatai Zvi's hedonistic followers, and the ascetic strength of the enduring and unlearned virtuous or the stern pious rabbis. Yasha Mazur plays a variety of roles and is responsive to a great variety of other people, constituting the Jew as Everyman, Singer's Leopold Bloom. And his harem tempts him in suitably varied ways: his wife, to the domestic Jewish idyll of "Short Friday"; Magda the peasant, to the civilizing and dominating fantasies of *The Slave*; Zeftel the Jewish whore, to modern revelry in depravity, the ultra-popular delights of Singer's Warsaw crowd scenes; and the intellectual Polish noblewoman Emilia to the great danger of *Moskat* and *The Manor*, conversion from the Faith to assimilation and secular prominence. Ironically, she is the concluding commentator: at the turn of the century, enlightened European Christianity applauds the Jew in his finest role, the scapegoat who can take on his ascetic shoulders the world's sins. Since we know the lurking horror, this final touch unites with the diminished echo of the epilogue to *Crime and Punishment* to provide Singer's best novel with the most sensitive and embracing irony of all his endings: a portrait of an uncertain penitent for an uncommitted crime, served by a devoted wife doomed to no reward.

Like the novels but with even more concentrated effect, the short stories vibrate with implications of allegory and archetype. On some rare occasions, as in "The Old Man" or "The Little Shoemakers," the allegory is overt. In the latter, Abba, a righteous shoemaker, tells his wife not to re-do the house—or Jewish revivalist faith—which has been standing since the seventeenth century, though it is in bad repair. He consciously identifies with patriarchs: "When his wife, Pesha, read to him, of a Sabbath, from the Yiddish translation of the stories in the Book of Genesis, he would imagine that he was Noah, and that his sons were Shem, Ham, and Japheth. Or else he would see himself in the image of Abraham, Isaac, or Jacob." After escape from the Nazis and a hitch as Jonah across the Atlantic, he manages even in the chaos of America to find a path to orderly workmanship for himself and his rich children, who are pounding away at lasts on their suburban estates as the story ends.

Generally, however, the timeless archetype rather than collapsed history works best for Singer. "The Gentleman from Cracow," for example, enacts in little the horrors of the catastrophic novels. The stranger who comes joyfully and wealthily into town insists, against both human judgment and the ritual which embodies divine law, on wholesale weddings. Such an attitude bespeaks the devil, and the inevitable result of the mass celebration is a conflagration in which all the town babies perish: as in the Bible and orthodox folk wisdom, the catastrophe is the punishment of the children for the sins of the parents—or, since Singer's devils are confessedly objectifications of human motives, our holy capacities for joy have been sacrificed to prideful lusts. "The Destruction of Kreshev" is a similar parable, in many ways an echo of *Satan in Goray*. Again the trouble in the small, hidden, orthodox community comes from without, with the arrival first of a pious but ignorant businessman and his family and then of Shloimele, the corrupt intellectual who does the devil's work. Frivolously, he destroys his wife's fruitful and healthy trust, giving her in adultery to Mendel the coachman, in effect uniting the creative energies of the folk not with the spiritual seminal Messiah but with the chaos of savage human nature.

It is obvious then that Singer forces on us in most situations a large, general reading, as well as an evocation of specific people named Moskat or Fischelson or Gedaliya. Such an approach entails some distance from the characters, whom we observe along with the author; our sympathy, if it exists, is perhaps a moral rather than an emotional one. With Singer, we are rarely in the midst of tragic emotional identification or on the height of comic understanding; we are somewhere in between, sometimes closer to one and sometimes to the other. We are unlikely to care very much whether Asa Heshel or Clara Jacoby will treat lovers kindly or cruelly or love or frustrate them at a given moment; whatever we feel for them depends on our identity as the Modern Jew in Uncertainty about Love or Faith, or the Modern Intellectual in that position, or more poignantly Man torn by his Uncertainties, or more bitterly human beings who have survived the Nazis but cannot forget them or what they did and meant. We can therefore, I think, come nearer to feeling for the less precisely circumstanced characters, as in the other three novels or in short stories like "The Shadow of a Crib," where dream or fantasy formally asserts the supernatural. While intensity combines with our acceptance of likeness in the very strangeness of such stories, in some like "Spinoza" that are closer to comedy, complexity of tone —wryness and sympathy and jest—derives also from distance, even from superiority to the characters. We are not, as in *Moskat*, painfully aware of our substitutes rushing about like antelopes surrounded by lions, the conclusions foregone; we are observing, as fairly ripe adults, what is to be salvaged from the confusion of life.

Usually, the life examined in Singer's narratives is presented in antithesis: either his pattern character needs to choose between two worlds or he may be balanced against an anti-type. Often these alternatives are objectified in one or more people, as in Dr. Fischelson and Dobbe, or Dr. Fischelson and the mass of society below him. Sometimes schizophrenia is implied ("Yentl the Yeshiva Boy"); sometimes a body is separated from its soul ("The Fast"), or a man is significantly buried between two women (*The Slave*, "Esther Kreindel the Second"), or a face is divided by the way light hits it (Abram Shapiro, Rechele, etc.), or a character is shown as living between two worlds:

an unbelieving Jew like Yasha Mazur, a resuscitated corpse like "The Man Who Came Back," the Marxist daughter of a convert, and so on. Dr. Fischelson, not a pious Jew and not an unbeliever, not a traditionalist and not modern, fittingly lives in a garret from which he looks up at the serene and ordered sky of moon, planets, and stars, and down at the fiercely passionate world of the slum.

In a middle state which has not even managed to remain a recognizable isthmus, Singer's man exhibits antitheses enough for a Gulliver-Faust. Willy nilly and namby pamby and helter skelter, he shifts fluidly between heaven and hell; aloofness and involvement; reason and emotion; science and poetry; the sacred and the profane; death and life; serenity and violence; aristocracy and the mass; philosophy and life; male and female; the unexpected and the habitual; spontaneity and calculation; speculation and faith; human will and animal nature; control and excess; order and chaos. Of these pairs, the most steadily important is that of order and chaos, the poles which in the less ambiguous stories determine the vision to be apocalyptic (*Satan in Goray* or *The Family Moskat*) or messianic (*The Slave* or "The Letter Writer"). The distinctions between chaos and order in the external world of nature, in the appearance of such human creations as city slums, in man's society, in man's mind—these all become aspects of the central question whether there is some union between men and the infinite or not. But order and harmony include the qualities of chaos which are attractive, particularly the calls of life in the slum, the variety or richness of humanity. Given the choice between limitation and order on the one hand and profusion and chaos on the other, Singer's living characters—particularly penitents like Yasha the magician—will choose the first.

But Singer's preference, where the crisis in the mind is not so intense, lies with the union of opposites rather than the rejection of one complex for the sake of the other. In most divisions less decisive than that between order and chaos, harmony is the ideal. And there are many such divisions.

To look through Singer's fiction is to catalogue the fusion or disintegration of oppositions. In *Satan in Goray*, Rabbi Benish and Reb Mordecai, the aloof intellectual and the charismatic zealot, fight over the fate of the congregation, and are replaced by their heightened psychological emanations, the important Itche Mates and the wild hedonist Gedaliya, whose captor and prey in one is the possessed symbol of Jewish humanity, Rechele. In *The Slave*, which monotonously insists on such contrasts as civilization and barbarism, Jew and gentile, depravity and the Law, the wife is given two names to symbolize her different aspects, and a miracle ties her to Jacob after their death. Yasha the Magician, while at home with an immense variety of people, is fundamentally an outsider, unsettled and undomesticated, who has however been given an "only support" and tie to stability in his wife. A master of physical laws and picker of physical locks, he is changed forever by a lock which has become the focus of psychological-spiritual forces. Asa Heshel of *Moskat*, Singer's most realistically complex embodiment of modern man, is of course aware of human division and its consequences: "His own nature remained a riddle to him. According to Spinoza, joy could be achieved only in community with others, yet he, Asa Heshel, avoided mankind." By comparison, Abram seemed to Asa integrated, a relic of a healthier past: "He knew how to live and how to die. He still had in him those juices which nourished the people in all the dark hours they had endured." But

Singer cannot accept unambiguously this sort of romantic moral food: where Asa is drawn toward the sterile, the dead, the idea of death, Abram, repudiating spirit for body, is too much of this world: "even admitting that there was such a thing as paradise, what good would it be to him? He'd rather have the Warsaw streets than all the wisdom of a Jewish paradise." Like all the other sensitive people in Singer's fiction, Asa and Abram know that life and death, body and spirit / mind should be one, but they cannot manage the union. The saints like the Tereshpol rabbi or Jochanan of Marshinov can be beacons, partial models, but not leaders; in their union with God they offer only earthly renunciation, which cannot nourish most bodies.

The natural tendency in man, then, is toward division, which from another viewpoint is the duality which demonstrates chaos, the desolating separation between instincts or between people or between God and man. The only affirmation in Singer's fiction is the experience of unity. And this experience of unity —which may be manifest in a vision of heaven or in an unconscious experience of love—is the miracle, the coming of the Messiah, that which fuses the opposites of ordinary experience into its transcendance, that which changes the quality of living.

Perhaps because this is the mode of certainty for Singer, his writing is full of visions, though they are visions of evil as well as of good. The sense of certainty may be concentrated in a certainty of hell as it may in a certainty of heaven. In some cases, as in "The Spinoza of Market Street," there may be actual visions and delusions, used like other technical devices to indicate a change in the state of a character. Before his meeting with Dobbe, for example, when the World War dislocates Dr. Fischelson's private world by delaying his pension, his illness includes an ominous, chaotic, apocalyptic dream-vision of his childhood which leads him to decide that "this earth belongs to the mad." From Rechele's ravishment by the Profane in *Satan in Goray* and Hindele's paranoia in "The Black Wedding," through Hadassah's technicolor nightmares after her attempted flight and Yasha's awareness of hell in a slum saloon, to the walking corpses looking into the Pit, Singer's work abounds in such apocalyptic visions. Whether he enlists our pity or sympathy or contempt through the device, it is invariably a sign of painful awareness of alienation, of a sense of sin or loss.

Other visions, unions, even penitential withdrawals can be vitiated, or at best rendered ambiguous, if they are primarily self-seeking rather than attempts to unite the self with an ordered world. Self-gratification through asserting pride or raising pleasure above all other goals destroys the good. These disorderly urges combine in the apocalypses, where inevitably the creative possibilities of decent humanity, as represented primarily by young women like Hadassah Moskat, are destroyed by prideful intellectuals, zealously aloof pietists, and desperate hedonists. If *both* Chillingsworth and Dimmesdale are corrupt, what hope for Hester, particularly if she is drawn to a drunken Reb Gedaliya?

Less thoroughgoing chronicles of moral failure, like "The Shadow of a Crib" or "The Unseen," tend also to focus on deficiencies of compassion. As these stories suggest, without the vital fusion of the genuine vision —the miracle—the corrupting pressures of the self can be kept in salutary check, in both individual and society, only by the traditional restraints and orthodoxies. While Singer's modern awareness, manifesting itself in ambiguity and irony, qualifies his traditionalism, he often sees no other alternative to suicidal selfishness. Even in children's stories, as for example "Grandmother's Tale" in *Zlateh the Goat,* Singer works to inculcate the old rules (as against, say, the intended iconoclasm of Thurber's fables). Though Singer claimed, in both the *Commentary* interview and *In My Father's Court,* to prefer his mother's intellectualism to his father's faith in tradition, where there is no adequate vision he insists on forms as the only protection against savagery. Even if Freud's *ego* is not vital enough to satisfy Singer's view of the spirit's needs, in the absence of such satisfaction he unhesitatingly supports the *superego* against the *id,* for society's sake.

Evidently, various ways exist of responding to the division inherent in life, some better than others, some vile because determined only by sensual or psychological gratification, others blessed by a source in humility or a deference to the Law. Best of all, however, is the positive experience of revelation, of miracle, when the senses and the will and the intellect unite in a spontaneous vision of harmony for the self and the universe—when, indeed, the Messiah comes. Man, however, is sometimes unable to tell when this miracle is occurring, or to remain in the condition of transcendence, or to distinguish the reality of miracle from its appearance. In "The Shadow of a Crib," for example, the important miracle does *not* occur. The proud Helena's kissing Dr. Yaretzky's hand, "one of those mysteries, one of those imponderables, which confound human reason," like Dobbe's showing the trousseau, constitutes a spontaneous exposure of oneself; but unlike the old scholar, the young physician does *not* complete the miracle by responding humanely. He is given a second chance, a vision of the faith and love of the old rabbi and his wife, which persuades him that the world is ordered, not chaotic. On the strength of this vision of possible harmony he proposes marriage, thereby saving Helena's life, but as the wedding approaches his prideful intellect sends him off. Like Asa Heshel, he repudiates the identity of human union and universal meaning, lacking the faith which should lead to the propagation of another human being. Therefore, his ghost haunts the spot where his and Helena's potential child—the miraculous symbol of their union—would have slept. Here the perverse intellect robs a basically good man of his vision; but in "A Piece of Advice," in "Gimpel the Fool," in "The Little Shoemakers," in "Joy" the miracle occurs and illuminates a life.

No such miracles can prevent the apocalypses even if, as in *Satan in Goray* and *The Family Moskat*, man desperately awaits transformation. Both books lead to Hartz Yanovar's horrifying conclusion, " 'Death is the Messiah,' " at least partly because man is unworthy. But even such a vision may be ameliorated. In "A Wedding in Brownsville" death is indeed the Messiah, for death is genuinely a unifier which confirms the spiritual community. In this literal modern elaboration of the *Zohar's* stories of good men escorted through death to paradise by their dead families, Dr. Margolin's consciousness carries him from his fatal accident to the wedding. At the hall, he sees the long-dead Raizel, his first love, in a crowd of all the dead and living, " 'as if the Messiah had come, as if the dead had come to life!' " And in these terms he is right: the line between death and life has disappeared, and with it all the divisions of guilt and innocence, youth and age, hope and frustration. The last of the vision is the bride and her father "with measured step" approaching the symbolic wedding canopy, and the night of Margolin's death is the happiest.

For Dr. Fischelson the false visions both of destruction and of Spinozist harmony provide fundamental ironies: in his life before the illness and wedding, he at times ran up on his short legs to peer out his window and sensed himself a part of the cosmos, a part of the divine and therefore eternal: "In such moments, Dr. Fischelson experienced the *Amor Dei Intellectualis* which is, according to the philosopher of Amsterdam, the highest perfection of mind." But the phrasing, the picture, above all Dr. Fischelson's loneliness, emphasize the shallowness of the impression and the delusiveness of the harmony. When Dobbe is so excited by his attention that she brings her trousseau to show him, that episode ends with her blush and his smile: preliminaries to an epiphany we are prepared to share, since it will make meaning of their lives as the view of the sky will not. Again, his union with Dobbe is his reunion with the Jewish—human—mass, with mankind, as her former employer reminds him: " 'We are all brethren now.' " Despite Dr. Fishchelson's Spinozist rejection of the supernatural, a true miracle has occurred through their mutual kindness. As they love, he is united not only to her and to mankind, but also to his youth and his early dreams. Dim recollections of romantic poetry (projections of the eternal and therefore unifying emotions in art) become clear and audible, and she responds with mysterious slang endearments. Miraculously he is made whole, virile, and healthy, and he falls "into the deep sleep young men know" and dreams himself in the Swiss mountains. Wordsworth's rainbow has become an old man's orgasm, but then as everyone says we are in the twentieth century.

Dr. Fischelson and Dobbe, particularly the more sensitive old scholar, have achieved a vision of felicity, arising from good will and receptivity, manifesting itself in a sexual display and a sense of union. At least for awhile—all the given eternity contained in the story—the wedding in "The Spinoza of Market Street" is a genuine one, a union of the forlorn, brought together by human kindness and concern, and at least for the time miraculously restorative. They are not the best conceivable representatives of Jewry or mankind but in 1914 they are also far from the worst: an elderly intellectual too modern for orthodoxy but too sane for frenzies like communism, still with enough faith to respond to his partner, a homely, shopworn, but warm and hopeful symbol of the folk. Their sexual miracle is no mere machinery or repellent perversity; through it, they can still affirm the possibility of a future.

The concluding irony, though justified by the ages and conditions of the lovers (and of the world), is also a revelation of man's inability to understand his own mind, a comic version of Yasha's intense confusion in *The Magician*:

> Yes, the divine substance was extended and had neither beginning nor end; it was absolute, indivisible, eternal, without duration, infinite in its attributes. Its waves and bubbles danced in the universal cauldron, seething with change, following the unbroken chain of causes and effects, and he, Dr. Fischelson, with his unavoidable fate, was part of this. The doctor closed his eyelids and allowed the breeze to cool the sweat on his forehead and stir the hair of his beard. He breathed deeply of the midnight air, supported his shaky hands on the window sill and murmured, "Divine Spinoza, forgive me. I have become a fool."

But what Spinoza can teach Dr. Fischelson is a distant faith in order, pointless acceptance of a cosmic harmony which negates both the individual and society (the cosmic order is undisturbed by the World

War). Spinoza's fool is our Gimpel, a triumphantly living human being. Through foolish involvement in passion, the alienated has joined the communal pattern, the intellectual has joined the firm humanity of the folk, the elderly and ailing has become at least touched by his own youth—and in ratification the divine, or supernatural, or God, or Higher Power (Singer's phrases in the interview) has provided the mystery of a restored virility. Union has triumphed over Spinozist assurance of emptiness.

Of course, Dr. Fischelson is a weak man casily deluded by pride of intellect, and his concluding self-reproach is Singer's ironic distancing of him and his experience. A voice seems to call, "Well, Fischelson, you'll never learn what's good." But while he cannot, like the recent Gombiner of "The Letter Writer," accept the fullness of his miracle, he has had faith and warmth enough for it to happen. At least at this stage of Singer's vision, the miracle cannot last, except perhaps for saints like Gimpel or Abba; it is followed by an absurd descent to intellect, as with Dr. Fischelson, or by a preserving death, as in "Short Friday" or "A Wedding in Brownsville." Nonetheless it is hopeful. Dr. Fischelson's miracle avers that in the midst of folly we can be saved by humanity and faith, almost any faith which does not conflict with humanity—and this is a long advance in faith from *Satan in Goray* and *The Family Moskat*.

# Moral Grotesque and Decorative Grotesque in Singer's Fiction

MAXIMILLIAN E. NOVAK

In one section of the memoirs of his youth, *In My Father's Court*, Isaac Bashevis Singer mentions that during a period of isolation he spent his idle moments drawing "freakish humans and fantastic beasts." It was at that very time that he discovered his first true delight in literature—Dostoevsky's *Crime and Punishment*. The conjunction of these events might be casual, but they suggest something significant about his later writing. Of *Crime and Punishment* he wrote that it reminded him of the Cabbala, and his response to Dostoevsky's unique combination of psychological insight, eccentric characterization and a realism undercut by fantastic dreams are perfectly apparent in his longest novel, *The Family Moskat*; but with the exception of that novel and *The Manor*, Singer's novels and stories are haunted by a vivid literary rendering of those "freakish humans and fantastic beasts" he drew when he was a child. Though he is capable of creating a Poland with as much realism as Dostoevsky's Russia, he usually renders the psychological and moral nightmare that lies beneath the surface of the action and character in Dostoevsky's fiction in terms of human or demonic grotesques, more reminiscent of Hieronymus Bosch or Max Ernst than of the Russian novelist.

Though much has been written about the psycho-

logical effect of the grotesque in art and literature—
the feeling of alienation caused by the combination of
the terrifying and the ludicrous—few have discussed
the particular techniques associated with the grotesque in fiction or attempted to see why a writer like
Singer might be different from other writers we asso-
ciate with the grotesque: Poe, Dickens, Kafka, and
Mann. The very disparity of such a list might make
one pause before trying to lump them together. To
see what Singer does with his demonic world, it might
be useful to take one of his less typical stories, a story
called "Alone," set not in seventeenth-century Poland,
where demons may be looked upon as part of the
technique of historical realism, but in the present and
at, of all places, Miami Beach. It might be thought
that the "terrible grotesque," as Ruskin called that
part of the form which involved a sense of spiritual
horror, would hardly show its face in such a place, but
Singer's Miami Beach is as haunted as his small Polish
villages.

The narrator tells how the "Hidden Powers" or an
"imp" must have heard his wish to be transported
from the midst of the noisy hotel where he was stay-
ing to some hotel where he could be alone. Next
morning the impossible happens: his luxurious hotel
shuts down, and he yields to a certain miserliness to
take an uncomfortable and ill-smelling room at $2.00
a day in a hotel presided over by a strange, hunchbacked Cuban girl. He lies in the sun, fantasizing over
the possibility of a woman moving into the hotel and
brooding over the eternal questions of God and existence. The isolation he sought suddenly becomes op-
pressing, and he decides to take a walk in a world
which has become truly alien to him. The human
beings around him assume the appearance of automa-
tons while inanimate objects appear human. The co-

conuts seem to hang from the trees "like heavy testicles," the parrots scream with human voices, a recently caught fish testifies to the chthonic forces in the universe. With the coming of the hurricane everything seems to writhe with life, while he can only see himself in a "half-dissolved image" reflected in the mirror like the divided form in a cubist painting. At the height of the storm, the hunchbacked girl materializes first like a ghost, and then as some kind of monster: "I saw her sitting in the chair, a deformed creature in an overlarge nightgown, with a hunched back, disheveled hair, long hairy arms, and crooked legs, like a tubular monkey." Gradually she takes on the recognizable demonic form of vice. He had dreamed of himself as another Boas, of a Ruth coming to him, and instead found himself besieged by the "forces of darkness still in possession of their ancient powers":

> Something in me cried out: *Shaddai*, destroy Satan. Meanwhile, the thunder crashed, the seas roared and broke with watery laughter. The walls of my room turned scarlet. In the hellish glare the Cuban witch crouched low like an animal ready to seize its prey— mouth open, showing rotted teeth; matted hair, black on her arms and legs; and feet covered with carbuncles and bunions. Her nightgown had slipped down, and her wrinkled breasts sagged weightlessly. Only the snout and tail were missing.

Sensing that he is confronting the temptation of Lilith, the narrator refuses her advances, and the hurricane passes.

Most writers would not fail to have the morning light reveal the absurdity of the situation, and the narrator does awaken with a cold sore. But how are we to read the end which informs us that the woman was "a witch who had failed in her witchcraft, a silent partner of the demons surrounding me and of their cunning tricks"? There is much in this demon-haunted world of Singer which recalls Kafka; there is something of the same sense of detail, and surely the image of Ketev Mriri in "The Gentleman from Cracow" with his eye in his chest, his serpentine tail and revolving horn might remind one of Kafka's famous cockroach. But the fact is that the demonic in Kafka seems to open the abyss into the "estranged world" that Wolfgang Kayser regarded as the key to the grotesque, while Singer's use of the grotesque confirms the reader in the sense of the reality of evil in the world. Indeed, in a larger sense, his demonic figures are symbols of the world and worldliness, and more often than not, Singer's treatment of the grotesque is put at the service of his moral vision. There are comic demons in Singer's stories but no moral ones, and this is why Singer's demons occasionally recall Bunyan rather than Poe, why he is often closer to the grotesque associated with Judaeo-Christian allegory than to the literary grotesque of nineteenth-century romanticism.

While there can be no question that Singer's techniques are literary in their origin and intent, what is perhaps most surprising is how thoroughly he has explored all facets of the grotesque. It is not surprising, however, that painters of the grotesque from Bosch to Grünwald, from Callot to Max Ernst, have chosen to paint a Temptation of St. Anthony. The painter of the grotesque selects the subject matter that will give him the best opportunity to display his talents and interests. As we shall see, there are times when Singer writes in the manner of such painters and appears to fit into Kayser's final definition of the grotesque as an "attempt to invoke and subdue the demonic aspects of the world," but at other times Singer can emphasize the ludicrous elements in the grotesque. There is little of John Ruskin's "noble grotesque" in the delightful autobiographical sketch, "Why the Geese Shrieked," in which a spiritual phenomenon accepted by Singer's father turns out to be amenable to the rationalistic explanations of his mother and reduced to the absurd and commonplace fact of wind making a noise as it rushes through the windpipes of some dead geese. In both this story and "Alone" there is a play with the demonic, but the one is comic and the other terrifying. Both are grotesque, but they are at opposite ends of the scale.

Probably the best example of Singer's pleasure in a purely decorative form of the grotesque is the story, "Cunegunde," which is little more than an exercise in that kind of horror which is usually associated with Hoffman and Poe and which has as its basic component the kind of pleasure in monsters, rats, snakes, and hairy plants that appears in such early forms of grotesque painting as Raphael's grotesque designs. The main character is a witch who appears in some of his other stories, and the tale exists almost entirely for its visual effects:

> Small and thick, she had a snout and eyes like a bull dog's, and a broad grisly chin. White hairs sprouted from the warts on her cheeks. The few strands of hair remaining on her head had twisted themselves into the semblance of a horn. Corns and bunions crowded her nailless toes. Cunegunde looked about her, sniffed the wind, frowned, "It's from the swamps," she murmured. "All pestilence and evil come from there."

Her mouth is "frog-like," she enjoys watching animals tortured, and she lives by devouring cats, dogs, and mice. She prays to devils and curses her enemies to death, and she, in turn, is finally beaten and stamped to death by a villager, dying surrounded by demons who rush at her with a "vengeful joy." It is a tribute to Singer's powers that he can transform such material into a powerful sketch. Singer's devils are a far cry

from Dostoevsky's sophisticated, poor relation, Ana-
tole France's witty companion or Shaw's bourgeois
man of sensibility. They are real and vivid, even where
their function is more or less to evoke horror for
horror's sake.

Though the murder of Cunegunde seems to be
little more than an added decoration, there are other
stories that combine this kind of horror with the psychological terror achieved by tracing the thoughts of a
murderer in the manner of Dostoevsky. The short
story, "Under the Knife," takes us into the mind of
the main character, Leib, as he plots his scheme to
take revenge on his former wife, Rooshke. Here Singer
has one of his rare exercises in the grotesque as Kayser's "play with the absurd." As Leib murders a whore
in preparation for murdering Rooshke, he kills what
seems to be an aged version of his former wife, and
then, while being shaved by Rooshke's present husband, a barber, he learns that he has murdered the
wrong woman, Rooshke's older sister. Within such a
story, Singer heightens his effects with his customary
use of caricature. The murderer has a missing eye, a
pockmarked face, and a sunken mouth. The whore
has only a few teeth left, and they are rusty and
crooked; her eyes are yellow. The murdered sister is
described as flabby and yellow-skinned with bulging
eyes and false teeth. If, as Luckacs argues convinc-
ingly, Kafka creates a world of remarkable detail to
make reality uncertain, Singer distorts the real world
to suggest the evil nightmare that lies about us as an
emanation of our fallen, sinful world. The Talmud
would provide ample material to explain why Singer
might want to create an image of the world which is
at times horribly real and horribly ugly; what is important for our purposes are the skillful literary methods
used to render that reality.

Singer never engages in the wildly comic distortions

of reality that one finds in Gogol's "The Nose," with its remarkable ability to convince us of an absurd world in which noses may go about disguised as minor government officials. His approach is far more traditional, and for this reason Ruskin's rather old-fashioned approach to the grotesque is often more helpful than Kayser's psychological analysis. For Ruskin sees in what he calls the "noble grotesque" a full realization of sin and death, and this is almost always what Singer is about, whether in his supernatural or realistic stories. His rendering of such themes in his stories has sometimes been discussed in terms of the supernatural folk tale, and it is true that demons are often recognizable as those who appear in the traditional Chassidic tales. But the resemblance stops there. Singer's demons are described in such a way as to evoke the grotesque. The demon-haunted world evoked in those stories is narrated by demons, as in "The Last Demon," "The Unseen," "Zeidlus the Pope," "From the Diary of One Not Born," or "The Destruction of Kresheve." But it is not so much these occasionally comic demons with their geese-like feet or spider-like form that make Singer a writer of the grotesque so much as his ability to make them seem real through grotesque description. And once we acknowledge their reality, we become aware of the sense of sin inherent in the external world. Though one of Singer's holy men dies with the statement, "I want you to know that the material world has no substance," Singer will often fill that insubstantial world with demons. Often his characters have but to take one step in the direction of sin, a step allowed to man by the freedom of the will, to plunge into that nightmare world of grotesque evil, which finds its best artistic archetype in the free artistic play in the paintings of St. Anthony's temptation by Bosch and Callot.

In these paintings the figure of St. Anthony is barely to be seen, and by his inner concentration he is able to avoid giving attention to the monsters that surround him. Singer will often use such temptation themes, whether in a story set in the visitable past, like *The Magician of Lublin,* where the demonic is reduced to the symbolic by a realistic surface, or in a story like "The Mirror," where a demon is the narrator. A comparison between the two shows that the line between his realistic fiction and his tales of the supernatural is not at all so clear as might at first be supposed. The demonic narrator of "The Mirror" tells how he tempts a beautiful and vain young wife in much the same way that Eve was tempted by the snake. The mirror, a rather familiar symbol in Singer's stories, is cracked, but the decoration of the frame, of "snakes, knobs, roses, and adders," is traditional grotesque ornament and prepares us for the entrance of the temptor. The demon catches her at the moment that she is admiring her breasts. He comes in a form similar to that in Dürer's engraving, *Knight, Death and Devil*: "there I was, black as tar, long as a shovel, with donkey's ears, a ram's horns, a frog's mouth, and a goat's beard. My eyes were all pupil." Zirel's reaction to his ugliness is not so much horror as amusement. The tone of the temptation is comic, and there is even something ludicrous about the little creatures who will devour her in Gehenna (hell), the worm and the mouse.

The demon convinces her with little difficulty that she will be happier living in Gehenna, and a few ritualistic transgressions lead her to a world of playful devils:

> Devils stood in a circle wiggling their tails. Two turtles were locked in embrace, and a male stone mounted a female stone. Shabriri and Bariri appeared. Shabriri

had assumed the shape of a squire. He wore a pointed cap, a curved sword; he had the legs of a goose and a goat's beard. On his snout were glasses, and he spoke in a German dialect. Bariri was ape, parrot, rat, bat, all at once. . . . Zirel broke into lamentations. The sound roused Lilith from her sleep. She thrust aside Asmodeaus' beard and put her head out of the cave, each of her hairs a curling snake. "What's wrong with the bitch?" she asked. "Why all the screaming?"

"They're working on her."

"Is that all? Add some salt."

"And skim the fat."

The story ends with the demon's comment on the great fun that the demons have in torturing Zirel, and we withdraw from this scene of torture with the musings of the imp on the lack of promotion in Gehenna and on the eternal questions of the existence of God and a paradise.

Such a story may seem very different from *The Magician of Lublin,* which concerns a very real Europe just before the turn of the century, but it remains to be seen whether the grotesquerie of the real world is very different from Singer's vision of hell. The magician, Yasha Mazur, ends his life in the world by shutting himself off from that world in a closed cell. He finally comes to see that a "single step away from God plunged one into the deepest abyss." The moral is almost the reverse of what one finds in an existentialist novel like Camus' *The Stranger;* the hero flees from freedom and arrives at a spiritual state which is directly opposed to the atheistical freedom achieved by Camus' hero. Instead of creating a world alive with demons, Singer deliberately selects the world of the magician as illustrative of the grotesque in life. Yasha is surrounded by his animals, a non-human, chattering, whistling shrieking chorus, a living arabesque of snakes, peacocks, monkeys, and parrots. His helper is a Polish girl, who leaps to life in a few lines through Singer's capacity to create a grotesque character:

> She was in her late twenties but appeared younger; audiences thought her no more than eighteen. Slight, swarthy, flat-chested, barely skin-and-bones, it was hard to believe she was Elzbeta's child. Her eyes were grayish green, her nose snub, her lips full and pouting as if ready to be kissed, or like those of a child about to cry. Her neck was long and thin, her hair ash-colored, the high cheekbones roseola-red. Her skin was pimply; at boarding school she had been nicknamed the Frog.

When her brother would threaten to harm Yasha, she would "rear back and hiss and spit like a cat at a dog." Indeed, her brother is described as having "nostrils wide as a bulldog's."

The relationship of this grotesque description to the demonic world of Singer is obvious enough, though its moral implications are not often so clearly delineated as they are in *The Magician of Lublin*, where the grotesque is almost invariably used to suggest a sense of evil—the evil inherent in the world and the evil inherent in freedom. Yasha is himself a figure capable of grotesque treatment; he is not only surrounded by grotesque humans and his menagerie, but he is also a magician, a person suspected of possessing supernatural powers. He can jump and dance on a tight rope, actions which Jennings maintains are most characteristic of the grotesque because they are "most calculated to call forth fear alongside amusement." One also thinks of Mann's grotesque and demonic Mario with his ability to control the will of his audience through hypnotism. For all *his* hypnotic power, Singer's Yasha is actually dependent upon and controlled by the people around him. And for all his seeming moral and intellectual emancipation, Yasha is torn by ethical doubts and actually believes that when his attempt at theft fails, he has been defeated by "a dybbuk, a satan."

After the death of Magda, who is carried off to the morgue like a dead chicken, Yasha confronts the real world in the grotesque figure of a giant, whom he sees in a cafe. Yasha himself is small, and the image of the giant's rotted teeth, pockmarked face and pimpled nose, of his eyes rolling in a kind of mad ecstasy, brings on a crisis of despair—a sense of nausea toward life and the world. Yasha reacts to this by destroying his freedom. From being a man in love with five women (one practically a child and another a prostitute), he becomes an ascetic. From being a man who dreamt of omnipotence, of flying and achieving wealth and fame, he becomes a recluse, whose fame is achieved, ironically enough, by withdrawing from the world he wished to conquer by his will.

The grotesque continues to function in Singer's fiction, then, whether the world he creates is overtly demonic or that of the realistic novel. One quality which the longer works permit, however, is a peculiar contrast between the beauty of nature and the grotesque world of human being and city. This satisfies the contrast between the normative and the monstrous that Santayana thought essential to grotesque art, but in *The Magician of Lublin* such a contrast has an essential moral function. As he rides along with Magda in his wagon, Yasha observes the beauty of the country in summer and is made to exlaim, "Oh, God Almighty, You are the magician, not I! . . . To bring out plants, flowers and colors from a bit of black soil." Though Yasha is brought to question any kind of spiritual significance in the operation of nature almost immediately after his exclamation, nature is always present to him as a reminder of the "Hidden Powers" that may lie behind appearances. In his cell at the end of the novel, he can only see that very essence of the grotesque, "death and lechery," in human nature, but in the world of snow flakes that fall on his window sill, in all of the physical nature, he finds the hand of God.

The narrative technique of *The Magician of Lublin* forces the reader to this conclusion. We see the world through Yasha, and through him we discover its meaning. The use of the grotesque buttresses the moral conclusions. Such a work is very different from Singer's most massive work so far, *The Family Moskat*, in which there is very little use of the grotesque, and the distinction suggests that Singer only employs the grotesque when he wants particular effects. In *The Family Moskat* his emphasis is historical and external, the technique reminiscent of Tolstoy. The individual characters are seen as part of a larger pattern of change in the Jewish community of Poland from the beginning of the century to the Nazi invasion. Historical perspective is achieved by allowing brief flashes of insight into the minds of all the characters including anti-Semites. There is little comment on such momentary shifts in point of view and little to distinguish between the thoughts of the evil and those of Rabbi Dan as he regards the minds of those around him:

> This was the lower world, where Evil reigned. Where else would Satan build his fortress? . . . Even the Devil had his roots in the divine creation. The important thing was that man had free will. Every blemish would find its purification. Uncleanliness was in reality an illusion.

It is not at all clear that such thoughts represent any final solution. Singer is here attempting an objectivity reminiscent of the techniques of Flaubert or Chekhov.

There is much in *The Manor* that recalls the technique of *The Family Moskat*. Singer once more assumes a stance suggestive of a universal sympathy and sadness, but the attempt at objectivity is gone. *The Manor* uses historical change more as a metaphor than as a core of meaning. Historically the half-mad thief and murderer, the Polish aristocrat Lucian has his role in life with that of the pious, kindly Jew, Calman, but we are left without any question about where our sympathies should lie. And if Singer leaves us with a feeling like that at the end of *The Magician of Lublin*, that it may be possible for each man to create a small area in which he may achieve some kind of moral righteousness through self-enclosure, if we can see in Calman's "makeshift Synagogue" a mirror image of Yasha's cell, it is because in both works he has pictured the external world as ugly, demonic, and grotesque.

In *The Manor* Singer uses the grotesque in both scene and character. The servant, Getz, has "a nose shaped like a ram's horn"; Temerle has "round bird-like eyes"; Mrs. Frankel "was dark as a crow, had a beaked nose and black pouchy eyes rimmed with webs of wrinkles." Characters are quickly shaped into life by these animal grotesques or suddenly caricatured in their ugliness. Noses have warts and pimples; skin seems like swiss cheese. The death of the Rabbi of Marshinov is prolonged by a vision of Paradise followed by a sudden and horrible vision of Satan and his legions. Even in his novels of nineteenth-century Poland, then, the grotesque has become a kind of moral shorthand for describing a world gradually departing from an ancient ethical code.

But the fullest exploitation of the great themes of the grotesque—the demonic, the dance of death, the combination of the ludicrous and the terrible, strange contrasts of tall and short, youth and age, beauty and

decay—may be found in his two novels of the seventeenth century, *The Slave* and, more particularly,
*Satan in Goray*. Both occur in the period following
the Chmelnicki massacre of 1648 and continue to the
disastrous aftermath of the coming of the false messiah, Sabbatai Zvi, in 1666—a period of great suffering
and disappointed expectation. In both novels Singer
uses the grotesque to communicate his ethical preoc-
cupations with the grotesque nature of evil and the
possibility of finding some protection from this evil by
a rigid conformity to the religious belief and virtue.

Taken into slavery after 1648, Jacob, the hero of
*The Slave*, finds himself surrounded by the near-bes-
tial peasantry:

> These women were unclean, and had vermin in their
> clothes and elflocks in their hair; often their skins were
> covered with rashes and boils, they ate field rodents and
> the rotting carcasses of fowls. Some of them could
> scarcely speak Polish, grunted like animals, made signs
> with their hands, screamed and laughed madly. The
> village abounded in cripples, boys and girls with goi-
> ters, distended heads and disfiguring birth marks; there
> were also mutes, epileptics, freaks who had been born
> with six fingers on their hands or six toes on their feet.

Jacob's confrontation with nature in his labors among
the mountains surrounding the village enables Singer
to draw with even stronger lines than in *The Magician
of Lublin* the contrast between the beauty of nature as
an emanation of God and the grotesque humans who
people the area. On the one hand we have descriptions of the sunrise that are worthy of Chekhov and
which brings Jacob to believe that "God's wisdom was
evident everywhere," and on the other the terrible
facts of barbarism—the torture of Jewish children,
rape, murder, and pillage. The only spiritual leader in
the village is the decadent village priest, Dziobak, and

Singer takes care of his moral state with a brief grotesque description: "He was a short, broad-shouldered man; he looked as if he had been sawed in half and glued and nailed together again. His eyes were green as gooseberries, his eyebrows dense as bushes. He had a thick nose with pimples and a receding chin."

Jacob eventually accompanies a howling mob of these grotesques in a kind of *Walpurgisnacht* revel during which he undergoes feelings similar to those of Coleridge's Ancient Mariner. He follows them, holding his nose against the smell of putrefaction, horrified by the sounds of horses, dogs, and donkeys emitted by the men, and wondering about their humanity. At first he finds some consolation in the belief that such a race can only be cured by complete extermination and that God was justified in destroying entire nations. But he shrinks from violence. He almost kills a "pock-marked fellow with a face like a turnip grater," and is horrified by his act. Then he sees a "monstrous square-headed girl with a goiter on her neck . . . hands, which were as long as a monkey's and as broad as a man's, their nails rotted away," a girl whose feet are full of boils and have a demonic goose-like quality, and he feels an overwhelming compassion. He realizes that his "mooncalf" actually understands the horror of her condition, and from his confidence that he had solved his dilemma about Moses's destruction of so many people, Jacob is once more turned back upon his prayers and his faith.

Though *Satan in Goray* treats the same time and many of the same problems as appear in *The Slave*, Singer takes the opportunity to treat the reaction of an entire Polish *shtetl* to the tempting freedoms offered by the followers of the false messiah, Sabbatai Zvi. Jacob also succumbs to the new ideas offered by the cult, but there is nothing surprising in Jacob's response to the liberalizing aspects of the sect. We know how he thinks, and we see the world through his eyes. In *Satan in Goray* the canvas is larger and the shifting point of view allows Singer a wider variety of psychological insights. The novel begins with a description of Goray after the great massacre. Dogs tear at the limbs of dismembered carcasses. The town is a spiritual and visual wilderness. Singer provides a brief historical synopsis of the rebuilding of the town under Rabbi Benish Ashkenazi to the year 1666, the great year of wonders in all of Europe, the year which many predicted would bring the end of the world and the judgment. The world which Singer conjures up for us is one in which the miraculous is part of everybody's expectations, though the use of the grotesque makes us suspicious about the final results The first news of miracles is brought by a woman wrinkled "like a cabbage head" with a "ram's horn nose," and the leading member of the town defending Sabbatai Zvi as the true messiah is the crippled Mordecai Joseph, who dances with his crutch at the news.

But if the grotesque is used in association with the moral evil inherent in the new cult, the psychological heightening in dealing with life in Goray is of a kind that Singer usually reserves for favorite, Dostoevskian scenes of theft and violence. Rechele, the daughter of the man who used to be the town's richest citizen, may indeed be haunted by demons, but Singer describes with meticulous care the kind of psychological background that would make her capable not merely of believing in a demonic world but in being possessed by it. As a child she is persuaded by her grandmother that she is surrounded by demons and that the house is haunted. This lesson is reinforced by the outpouring of blood in the home of her uncle, Reb Aeydel Ber, a ritual slaughterer. Left alone in this house after the death of her grandmother, she sees or dreams of a nightmare world out of Hieronymus Bosch—a world in which the candle box may do a jig while the pots float about the room.

We can understand the psychological motivation which could produce visions in Rechele, but Singer gives concrete reality to these visions by his narrative method. The use of indirect discourse gives us Rechele's inner thoughts, while the third person narrative provides the illusion of objectivity. Sexually frustrated by her marriage to the impotent disciple of Sabbatai Zvi, Reb Itche Mates, Rechele begins to hear voices, and by a process long ago described by Swift in his *Tale of a Tub*, her suppressed sexuality finds an outlet in enthusiasm and prophecy. Her announcement that Reb Gedaliya is worthy "like Elijah, to behold the face of the Divine Presence" leads to the ritual slaughterer's entire domination of the town in the name of the new sect. He begins to reverse all the ethical teachings of the Talmud. He urges all the women to commit adultery, sleeps with Rechele, works cures by witchcraft, and finally plunges the entire town into evil. Singer takes the opportunity of some of his finest evocations of the demonic and the grotesque:

> A copper cross hung on his breast, under the fringed vest, and an image lay in his breast pocket. At night Lilith and her attendants Namah and Machlot visited him, and they consorted together. Sabbath eve, dressing in scarlet garments and a fez, like a Muslim he accompanied his disciples to the ruins of the old castle near Goray. There Samael presented himself to them, and they all prostrated themselves together before a clay image. Then they danced in a ring with torches in their hands. Rabbi Joseph de la Reina, the traitor, descended from Mount Seir to join them in the shape

of a black dog. Afterward, as the legend went, they would enter the castle vaults and feast on flesh from the living—rending live fowl with their hands, and devouring the meat with the blood. When they had finished feasting, fathers would know their daughters, brothers their sisters, sons their mothers.

The plunge into freedom is invariably a plunge into the demonic. The passage builds dramatically from the traditional grotesquerie of the witch's sabbath to complete moral degradation.

And while Gedaliya leads the town into sin, Rechele's holy voices are gradually replaced by an image of the profane which takes concrete demonic form. Eventually she dreams that she is pursued and raped by the devil:

A bearded figure pursued her, hairy and naked, wet and stinking, with long monkey hands and open maw. Catching her at last, he carried her as light as a feather (for she had all at once become weightless) and flew with her over dusk-filled streets and tall buildings, through a skyless space full of mounds, and pits, and pollution. At their back ran hosts of airy things, half-devil and half-man, pointing at them, pursuing them. The Thing swept her over steep rooftops, gutters, and chimneys, huge and mildewy; there was no escape. It was stifling and the Thing pressed her to him, leaned against her. The Thing was a male; he wanted to ravish her. He squeezed her breasts; he tried to force her legs apart with his bony knees. He spoke to her rapidly, hoarsely, breathing hard, imploring and demanding. . . . He threw her down and entered her. She cried a bitter cry, but there was no sound, and she started from sleep. With perfect clarity she saw that the dark house was crowded with evil things, insane beings running hither and thither, hopping as on hot coals, quivery and swaying, as though they were all kneading a great trough of dough.

The psychological power of terror implicit in waking from a nightmare to discover or believe for an instant that the dream is no dream at all is rendered brilliantly by Singer, but Rechele's experience is neither madness nor dream. Her vision has the feeling of concrete reality as well as a certain nightmarish, comic illogicality that makes it particularly grotesque. Rechele is frequently found to break into laughter.

Before the final chapter, Singer allows us to experience with Gedaliya the discovery of Rechele's possession, and we are not left to think that the blowing out of candles and the voice of Satan is merely a quirk of Rechele's tormented psyche. The treatment of the exorcism of the dybbuk, handled in terms of period demonology, confirms us in our belief that such a demon may indeed exist, though the fact that Reb Mordecai Joseph, who drove the holy Rabbi Benish out of Goray, is chosen as the hero of the "objective" account of the expulsion of the demon from the body of Rechele, may lead one to suspect a certain irony behind this report as it is seen within the total complex of events.

*Satan in Goray* is obviously so far superior to a story like "Cunegunde" that one might justly regard it of a different literary species. In the one, the grotesque takes on genuine moral significance, in the other it is little more than a kind of artistic play. But it is the impulse toward this particular kind of artistic decoration that lies behind some of Singer's finest efforts. A story like "Caricature" has no profound moral theme, but the grotesque portraits have a value of their own. Singer shows his protagonist, Dr. Margolis, looking with some distaste on his aging wife:

> She had grown smaller and smaller and puffier and puffier; her stomach stuck out like a Man's. Since she had practically no neck, her large square head just sat on her shoulders. Her nose was flat and her thick lips

and jowls made him think of a bulldog. Her scalp showed through her hair. Worst of all she had begun to grow a beard, and though she had tried to cut, shave, singe off the hair, it had merely grown denser. The skin of her face was covered with roots from each of which sprouted a few prickly shoots of a nondescript color. Rouge peeled from the creases of her face like plaster. Her eyes stared with a masculine severity.

This kind of sketch is what makes Singer such a magnificent writer of short stories, and it is within the short story that he exploits the full range of the grotesque: themes of disproportionate size ("Big and Little"), premature aging ("Esther Kreindel the Second" and "Three Tales"), confusion of sexes ("Yentl the Yeshiva Boy"). Sometimes Singer uses the grotesque for purely comic effect as in "Taibele and Her Demon," in which the teacher's helper, Alchonon, pretends to be a demon in order to have an affair with a widow, Taibele.

In his longer stories and novels, Singer has used the grotesque to express larger themes and given it a more significant function. Occasionally, this function is not very clear. In *The Slave*, for example, an old, crippled woman with a wart on her nose and hair on her chin proves to be completely saintly and teaches Jacob a lesson about the illusory nature of appearances. This is very different from the way the grotesque is used in *The Magician of Lublin*, but then Jacob is a man striving for an answer to his problems and often arriving at answers which are original and, perhaps, only suitable for himself. It should warn us that Singer is a novelist and short story writer, not a philosopher, and that the grotesque is a literary tool which he uses at his best, to lend significance to the world of his fiction and even in his slighter efforts, to provide a kind of excitement that few modern writers can match.

# Singer's Apocalyptic Town
## *Satan in Goray*

EDWIN GITTLEMAN

According to the old Jewish storytelling tradition, Chelm was a Polish town remarkable only because of the large number of fools who lived there. A well-known Chelm story is told about a pious and prosperous Jew who one day startled his wife by rushing into her kitchen and excitedly announcing that he had just learned from neighbors that the Messiah was coming and would arrive in their town within a few hours. Instead of being overjoyed by this prospect of the long-awaited "End of Days," the husband was distraught. He moaned and beat his breast. The wife was puzzled by his sorrowful reaction to this wondrous news until he reminded her that they had recently built a comfortable house, had invested all their hard-earned money in livestock, and had just finished planting their fields. She thought for a moment, and then her face brightened. "Don't despair!" she cried out joyfully. "Just think of all the calamities we Jews have endured throughout the ages. With the help of the good Lord we have managed to overcome the most dreadful tribulations. With just a little more help from Him we can overcome the Messiah, too!"

Comic ironies are the only imperatives in the legendary world of Chelm. No alternative to incongruity is possible. In Chelm, it must be absurd for anyone to construe the fulfillment of the Messianic promise as a terrible threat; it must be absurd too for anyone to consider invoking a merciful God for salvation from the Redeemer. Consequently, whatever may be the validities of the assertions of husband and wife, in Chelm they are displaced by pressures from a sense of genial if irreverent humor. But other worlds, other absurdities, other ironies, other pressures, other humors exist, and they exist nor far from those of Chelm.

A map of Poland would locate the town of Goray about fifty miles southwest of Chelm. Apparently unknown to Jewish storytellers before 1935 when its legendary potential was disclosed in *Satan in Goray*—a beautifully fashioned but nevertheless grotesque novel —Goray is where the pragmatic honesty of the Chelm couple would have been validated, and where it would have doomed them to martyrdom instead of folly. By conflating Messiah with Satan while excluding the Chelm couple, the fictional Goray contains and compresses their insights instead of discharging them through laughter, and consequently explosive tensions quite different from comic ironies are generated. A contrasting order of imperative prevails in Goray.

Only the space of fifty miles is necessary to position Chelm and Goray at opposite ends of the world. This short but sufficient distance allowed an anti-Chelmic system of fiction to be designed. Assertions there have dreadful consequences instead of simply providing amusing conclusions for anecdotes. It is, moreover, a fictive system within which a brilliant but subversive art is possible.

*Satan in Goray* was the first extended attempt by its author, and the most radical, to define himself as a writer of fiction. Son of the "unofficial" rabbi of Warsaw's Krachmalna Street, Isaac Singer willfully transformed the identity imposed upon him by his Chassidic father's rigid pieties, otherworldliness, and sustaining belief in wonder-working rabbis. This transformation required no act of repudiation. Although he became Isaac Bashevis, a prolific writer of Yiddish fiction instead of a faithful reader of sacred Hebrew texts, he renounced nothing and affirmed everything. Protected by accurately detailed memories of the Jewish culture he had experience and studied, he boldly created this more comprehensive identity for himself. He continued nevertheless to preserve a nominal relationship to his father by remaining Isaac (the not-quite-sacrificed son); however, by being Isaac Bashevis rather than Isaac Singer, he simultaneously correlated himself to Bathsheba, his devout but rationalistic and skeptical mother. She was the daughter of the *Mitnagid* (rationalist anti-Chassid) rabbi of Bilgoray.

The matronymic was dangerous for Isaac because self-exposing. Bathsheba—with its familiar form, Bashevis—had been a name shameful and shocking to the pious sensitivities of young Isaac Singer. It was "too suggestive of King David's sin." Later, at the time he deliberately chose "Bashevis" for his public signature, he understood that David's authority was bardic as well as regal, and that the powers of singer and sinner, however awesome individually, were mutually redemptive. Together they transcended the distinctions between sacred and profane, and they thereby determined the limits of his consciousness as a writer. Isaac Bashevis then, not Isaac Singer, was the discoverer of the fictional world of Goray and its orgiastic energies. At the same time, however, Goray allowed Isaac Singer to discover the possibilities of Isaac Bashevis. *Satan in Goray*, a Yiddish fiction-out-of fact published in Warsaw in 1935 and reprinted in Yiddish in New York in 1943, therefore records an act of double discovery.

*Satan in Goray* is an experimental novel whose dynamics are deliberately proto-novelistic. Its form is that of a long tale. But since it is a tale told by an aggressively historical imagination, it is a tale which quickly acquires momentum by selectively acquiring and structuring facts. It is a tale which, within the space of some two hundred pages, moves swiftly (and almost imperceptibly) from an archaic oral tradition of story to a more sophisticated scribal tradition. Beginning with a spoken recollection of the year 1648, the novel invests Goray with a fictive present for the years 1666–67, and finally (in the last two chapters) becomes a literary document whose emphatic last words are "CONCLUDED AND DONE."

The momentum of the form derives from an imagination which has brooded over the communal impact of two isolated historical events of the year 1648, has become obsessed and possessed by them, and must therefore now utter them in an effort to exorcize the demon consciousness it has internalized from the past. The historical events are these: in 1648 Bogdan Chmelnicki undertook a Cossack invasion of Poland, triggering peasant uprisings which ravished the countryside; and in 1648 an oriental Jew, Sabbatai Zvi, proclaimed himself Messiah and acquired a substantial following.

Not until these historical events were brought into imaginative conjunction with medieval Jewish culture could the fictional present of an anti-Chelmic Goray come into existence for 1666–67, and culminate in a disfiguring ritual of purification. This ritual was made necessary in 1666 by the apostasy of Sabbatai Zvi, the self-deluding Messiah.

The voice properly evoked by the historical imagination to narrate *Satan in Goray* is a tormented, intense, restless voice. It is the voice of a dybbuk, struggling with restraint, squirming to detach itself from the events of the story by means of its own expression. Although itself demonic—by virtue of being a human spirit displaced by death—this dybbuk knows only its own demonic experience. Consequently, while it can record the encounters with demons and similar supernatural beings which others report, it refuses to authenticate the accuracy of such marvelous reports. Neither affirming nor denying the objective existence of spirits and miracles, it nevertheless asserts their subjective reality for others. And so it is a wise dybbuk, prudentially wise, because of its skepticisms, and perhaps because its own private guilts are unconfessed. It is a wise dybbuk too because it seeks its own release from Goray by knowing and telling "the way of the world." What it knows and tells is that in 1667 Satan exists in Goray, and that "in time everything reverts to what it has been."

Through this narrative voice both Satan and Goray are experienced. They are experienced not only as a strange community in a fabulous geographical region but also as a proximate condition of mind with a familiar psychology. They do so because the year 1648 had been imaginatively comprehended as a year both of absolute desperation and of infinite hope. The terrifying irony of the novel is that, in time (that is, in 1666–67) the Messianic hope becomes infinitely more devastating and demoralizing than the total despair produced by the savage violence of Chmelnicki and his followers. They had merely "violated women and afterward ripped open their bellies and sewed cats inside."

The natural history of Goray is not natural at all. It is, according to the dybbuk-narrator, "the town that lay in the midst of the hills at the end of the world." Goray, therefore, is not *a* town but *the* town. And it is *the* town "at the end of the world," literally and figuratively. It is the town isolated from other settled places by topography and by eschatology. Its remoteness is absolute. Goray is the town on the edge, the marginal town, the town on the verge of falling into the void, the town whose existence is measured by its proximity to the cosmic cataclysm ending the world. It is *the* apocalyptic town.

Although deeply committed to ancient Jewish tradition and culture, Goray is the town whose distinguishing consciousness was shaped by the Chmelnicki terror, when it seemed as if Goray "had been erased forever." Its inhabitants in 1648 were either massacred or forced to flee to large cities not so close to "the end of the world." Not having experienced a time before Chmelnicki crossed the barrier of enclosing hills, Goray is effectively created by an act of destruction. Its beginnings are in catastrophe. It has no history until it is destroyed as a community. Its origin is in annihilation, and thus its birth is death. Although in possession of a traditionally Jewish communal memory and social structure, it has no functional past until it is totally devastated. The beginning of time in Goray coincides with its end. It acquires existence by being "erased," as if "forever." Goray is therefore formed and informed by being deformed. Deformation subsequently remains its special destiny.

Many years after the Chmelnicki devastation of Goray, surviving former inhabitants gradually return to the abandoned town, paint over the "blood-and-marrow splattered walls," re-establish a communal life, and thereby initiate a process which, in time, will cause the town to revert to what it had been before— the victim of shattering forces. Goray will be brought even closer to "the end of the world."

The most enervated and therefore potentially most dangerous of those returning from exile is Rechele. A

seventeen-year-old girl, she embodies the past and future of the town, like a cat sewed inside her. Born in
Goray in the fateful year 1648, she is the spawn of the
great devastation. Her biography is—and will be—the
history of Goray. A sickly child raised in the home of a
lusty, blood-splattering uncle who serves as the ritual
slaughterer for the Jewish community in Lublin, she
always had been terrified by the destructive energies of
her knife-wielding guardian. Rechele had grown into a
beautiful but alien being, a neurasthenic woman
whose psychic wounds have crippled her physically as
well as emotionally. But despite her instability and
her deformity, upon her return to her native place she
asserts her recognizably human nature. She "aroused
sinful thoughts in men." Moreover, "her large, dark
eyes gazed beyond the rooftops—wide-open, brilliant,
as though seeing things concealed from others."
Powerful but unfulfilled sexuality generates fearful,
incommunicable visions for this woman isolated by
secret unhappiness.

After the re-establishment of the community, in
1666–67 a series of "highly respectable" strangers sep-
arately visit the town, bringing amazing news from
the world beyond the hills. In Europe and the Near
East, miracles have been performed by Sabbatai Zvi.
With the arrival of Itche Mates, a Cabbala-learned
peddler and disciple of the Messiah, zealous millenari-
ans succeed in routing the scholarly but ineffectual
Talmudist who had always been the town's rabbi, and
gain control of Goray. At the same time Rechele
acquires a husband. But the ascetic Itche Mates
proves impotent, disappointing the Sabbateans and
intensifying the frustrations of Rechele.

Goray rejoices, however, at the arrival of a wonder-
working apostle of the Messiah who is qualified to fill
a ritual office vacant since 1648. Reb Gedaliya, before
coming to Goray, had been the ritual slaughterer in

Zamość, a city which seventeen years before had re-
pulsed Chmelnicki's attack. Rechele also rejoices.
With Reb Gedaliya's arrival she gains a virile lover
whom her tormented mind identifies with "the great
and awful Angel Sandalfon," the Angel of the World
who listens to the prayers of the faithful.

After being liberated from loneliness by her mid-
night communion with this world-mediating spirit,
Rechele publicly discloses prophetic powers which
confirm the Messianic calling of Sabbatai Zvi and
identify Reb Gedaliya as "a godly man, and worthy,
like Elijah, to behold the face of the Divine Presence." Her prophecy is exploited by the Sandalfon-
Gedaliya, who "hated sadness" and whose "way of
serving God was through joy."

In preparation for the new dispensation he exercises
apostolic authority by lifting traditional prohibitions
and modifying ancient customs. His reforms deform:
they deprive the community of the familiar supports
which had given coherence to its precarious existence.
A Dionysiac spirit prevails in Goray, corresponding to
Rechele's miraculous nighttime ecstasies. Rechele herself is adored by Sabbateans who come from distant
places to be sanctified by her prophetic presence.
"Goray, that small town at the edge of the world was
altered. No one recognized it any longer." For the first
time in its history a prosperous town, a town no longer
insulated by the surrounding hills, Goray (like Rechele) now is freely accessible to the world, to profane
as well as sacred impulses, to natural and unnatural
influences.

These new circumstances enable Reb Gedaliya to
complete difficult Cabbalistic calculations. He reveals
to Goray that

> the ram's horn would announce the coming of the Mes-
> siah in the middle of the month of Elul, and three days

before Rosh Hashana a cloud would descend and the pious would climb aboard and be off to the land of Israel. . . . Every godfearing man would have ten thousand heathen slaves to wash his feet and care for him. Duchesses and princesses would act as the nurses and governesses of Jewish children, as had been foretold in the Book of Isaiah; thrice daily the Jews would fly like eagles to the mount of the Lord and there bow and prostrate themselves before the Holy Temple. The afflicted would be healed, the ugly made beautiful. Everyone would eat from golden dishes and drink only wine. The daughters of Israel would bathe in streams of balsam, and the fragrance of their bodies would suffuse the world.

And Goray is convinced that redemption is imminent.

When the ram's horn fails to sound and the cloud fails to appear, Goray is totally demoralized. Unprepared for the winter season, townspeople suffer famine, storms, epidemics, and humiliation. It seemed, says the dybbuk-narrator, as if "evil spirits" now ruled Goray. The Chmelnicki holocaust had been less destructive. The town is divided between those who are outraged because they had been deluded, and those who stubbornly remain faithful to Sabbatai Zvi. Even in the study house, prayers are disrupted by wild and bloody attacks made by worshippers against each other.

The "triumph" of "the Evil One" is completed in Goray in 1667 when finally it is learned that in the previous year Sabbatai Zvi had been converted to Islam. The community becomes more embittered and further fragmented. Even the faithful Sabbateans are divided: one faction asserts that the Messiah will not appear until the present generation has become completely virtuous; the other faction claims that the Messiah will not appear until the present generation has become completely depraved. Goray therefore is torn apart not only by disillusionment but by ascetic Sabbateans intent upon self-flagellation, and by antinomian Sabbateans desecrating everything holy. Irrationality, disguised by pious rationale, prevails.

Corresponding to the saturnalian disintegration of communal order and traditional Law, the prophetic consciousness of Rechele becomes entangled with a nightmarish struggle between "the Sacred" and "the Profane," her hallucination continuing until the former is ritually slaughtered by the latter, and Rechele is ravished by "the Thing." Impregnated by her vision of Satan, she now actually nourishes a monstrous creature inside her.

> Rechele suffered extraordinary tortures. At times the evil one blew up one of her breasts. One foot swelled. Her neck became stiff. Rechele extracted little stones, hairs, rags, and worms from wet, pussy abscesses formed on the flesh of her thigh and under her arms. Though she had long since stopped eating, Rechele vomitted frequently, venting reptiles that slithered out tail first.

Knowledge of such a ferocious pregnancy reaches even the peasants in outlying areas. They now understand that in Goray "Satan has entered the body of a daughter of the Jews."

But even more significant than the final publication to the gentile world of the degeneration of Rechele-Goray is the sudden silence of the dybbuk-narrator at this climactic point in the novel. His sensible intelligence disappears rather than fails. He has succeeded in effecting his own release from *Satan in Goray* by annihilating himself, and thereby finding permanent rest.

The remainder of the novel derives from a quite different authority. The concluding two chapters purport to be a Yiddish translation from "the worthy book The Works of the Earth." It is an apocryphal account of an unnamed woman in Goray who had been possessed by a dybbuk, apparently written by an anti-Sabbatean Talmudist who lacks the restraining skepticism of the original narrative voice but possesses instead a Sandalfonic tone.

Time moves with agonizing slowness in this detailed account of how an abjuring Goray Sabbatean ("may his rememberance be a blessing"), ritually slaughters the woman (Rechele) by expelling the dybbuk (her Satanic fetus). With the painful delivery, the purified Rechele dies, her redemption proving unbearable. And the fictional Goray, similarly cleansed, ends its own beautifully crippled existence. At the expense of Rechele-Goray, the Satan-as-Messiah has been reborn and released into the world.

The explicit moral of the fragment from "The Works of the Earth" with which the novel ends, is:

> Let None Attempt To Force The Lord: To End Our
> Pain Within the World: The Messiah Will Come
> In God's Own Time: And Free Men of Despair
> And Crime: Then Death Will Put Away
> His Sword: . . .

While adequate as a "moral" for "The Works of the Earth," it scarcely is adequate for *Satan in Goray*—except as a brilliantly ironic conclusion for a novel which itself subverts such piously orthodox sentiments.

Isaac Bashevis Singer has made clear by writing *Satan in Goray* that the only God capable of coexisting with the universe which contains a town like Goray is either a God infinitely distant from it and whose outermost extremity is Satan, or else a God— like the dybbuk-narrator—who must withdraw from the universe into the silence of renunciation.

In the Goraic universe goodness is either ineffectual, irrelevant, or non-existent, while piety is an invi-
tation to demonic seizure, and innocence is valuable
only because it is capable of being corrupted. Even
though he never appears in Goray, and even though
his is the power of pretense, Sabbatai Zvi does exert an
influence upon Goray more crucial than that of God.
The power of Satan thus has a reality and an immedi-
acy which exceeds that of God. Although that Satanic
power is destructive, it nevertheless confirms the value
of existence in a way that the unexercised power of
God does not.

But if God is silent in Goray, His silence becomes
the sign of His presence, of His concern, and of His
subtle judgment on the miserable world of Goray.
The prayers of Goray's devout worshippers are unintelligible to God; were it otherwise, God in Goray
would be indistinguishable from Satan in Goray. The
intelligence of God is incomprehensible to the inhabitants of Goray; were it otherwise, God would not
exist except as the Goraic Messiah—a product of
defective human imaginations.

At novel's end, what remains is a Messianic hope of
a very special sort. It is a Messianic hope which is
valuable only because it is unfulfilled and unfulfilla-
ble, a hope which is justified so long as it is an unkept
and unkeepable promise. Goray may be the worst of
all possible worlds but it nevertheless is a world worth
preserving, so long as its hope remains an aspiration
rather than a reality upon which to base the conduct
of life. It need not be a world without value, however
great its depravities.

Since the immediate prospect of Messianic fulfillment deprives the Messianic hope of its value as a
redemptive force, a limitation of belief is necessary:
while the Messianic promise is to be believed, this

belief must include disbelief in the Messianic realization. In effect, then, the Messianic hope is a life-sustaining lie, one which makes continuing human experience possible.

Salvation, according to the Singer of *Satan in Goray*, is to be found in vision; that is, in vision which remains distinguishable from ordinary experience, in envisioning while remaining skeptical of the reality of vision, in possessing vision but not being possessed by it, in discriminating between vision-as-art and vision-as-life, in entertaining the Messianic dream instead of enacting the Messianic reality which will perform as an intolerable nightmare.

The justification for the Messianic hope, according to the Singer defined by *Satan in Goray*, is to be found in its element of threat, a threat which inhibits men from destroying the world by reserving that apocalyptic privilege for the Messiah who must never arrive: if He does, he must take the form of the Goraic Satan. This promise of redemption through the threat of Messianic destruction therefore has a practical salving power—so long as it never becomes the basis for human policy.

Salvation is to be found in preferring destruction to destroying, and victimization to victimizing. To elect to be sacrificed is to be ritually slaughtered, and thus makes possible the judgment, "Clean!" This is the only redeeming alternative to the intolerable actualities of Goray, and is the only "moral" extractable from the histories of Rechele and her dybbuk-narrator. It is a perverse and subversive "moral" which places Isaac Bashevis Singer, by virtue of his "imagination of disaster," in the American tradition of Edgar Allan Poe, Nathaniel Hawthorne, and Herman Melville, rather than in the East-European tradition of the Chelmic storytellers.

# The Family Chronicle as Paradigm of History
*The Brothers Ashkenazi* and
*The Family Moskat*

MAX F. SCHULZ

I. J. Singer's *The Brothers Ashkenazi* and Isaac Bashevis Singer's *The Family Moskat* illustrate the efforts
of two supreme artists to accommodate the conven-
tions of the familial epic to this century's agonizing
awareness of history. Each solves the problem of finding a form paradigmatic of history in a manner characteristic of his reaction to the Chassidic Warsaw milieu
from which he fled.

If we are to believe Isaac Bashevis's account of his
older brother in *In My Father's Court*, I. J. Singer
uncompromisingly rejected what he regarded as the
intellectual sterility and puritanical asceticism of the
ghetto. His reaction seems at the outset to control his
conception of *The Brothers Ashkenazi*. The tone of
the novel is coolly ironic. He sardonically details the
Jewish community's obsession with social standing; its
eager collaboration in the transformation of rabbis
from students of the sacred Law into sharpers at home
with "bills, percentages, profits, contracts, promissory
notes, and all the devices and tricks of the business
world"; and its easy sanction of the employer class's
economic exploitation of the worker in combination
with a hypocritical concern for his morality. The con-
tradictions between old-fashioned *shtetl* piety and en-

lightened commonsense particularly arouse I. J. Singer's jocularity; for example, he relates that Reb Abraham Hirsh Ashkenazi always visits his wonder Rabbi at Passover, armed with special *matzos* "made from flour which had been under guard from the growing of the grain until the baking of the cakes. . . . They were less digestible than ordinary matzos," Singer slyly adds, "but considerably holier." Such irony reduces the epical tone characteristic of the family chronicle and emphasizes instead, much as does Byron's poem *Don Juan*, that the literary world of the narrative is akin to the pedestrian, work-a-day world of reality. This de-emphasis of the traditional heroic treatment of the saga of three generations is underscored by a controlling animal metaphor, deriving from the biblical precept that "There is no difference between man and beast." The same reductive effect is at work in I. J. Singer's portrayal of the despicable personality of the protagonist Max Ashkenazi with the clinical detachment of an anthropologist reporting the characteristics of a new species.

The structure of the novel, however, represents Singer's greatest effort to remove his chronicle from the fabulous pattern of the genre. Not only does he diminish the patriarch to a minor role in the family in favor of the second generation, but he limits the progeny to two sons and concentrates his attention on one. This strategy turns the familial epic into a *Bildungsroman* of sorts. Furthermore, he parallels the growth of Max and Jacob Ashkenazi from Chassidic *cheder* pupils to industrial financiers, with the evolution of Lodz from a Jewish village of pious hand-loom operators to the Polish center of the weaving industry. In the merger of the destiny of the Ashkenazi family with the history of the supranational European business community, and its accompanying shift of lines of conflict from Jew versus Gentile to worker versus mercantilist, this dual tale of a family and of a city becomes a microcosm of the industrial revolution in Eastern Europe. Max Ashkenazi's effort to enhance the financial reputation of his name (that it is also the generic name of the Germanized, or Yiddish speaking Jews, as distinguished from the Sephardic, or Spanish-Portuguese speaking Jews, is significant) also becomes symbolic of the effort of East European Jewry to break out of its centuries' long isolation and enter the mainstream of Western history. In short, I. J. Singer harnesses his family chronicle to the events of the nineteenth and early twentieth centuries. Thus the narrative follows history rather than legend; it is closer to national than to mythic drama.

But by the end of the novel the pejorative tone toward both Max Ashkenazi and the Chassidic community has altered and the story has taken on epical dimensions. Through his superhuman labors in the textile industry, Max has made himself the industrial "king of Lodz." The small-statured, repulsive ex-Talmudic student, distrustful, perfidious, inhuman, is endowed in old age with heroic qualities, loyalty, pertinacity, integrity, wisdom, selflessness. Singer's irony still operates, but it has deepened and broadened in profundity. No longer Max and the Chassidim but man and the world are objects of its disillusionment. The pointlessness of Max's Herculean labors is laughed at—but only as part of the unaging vanity of all human endeavor. The final—and ultimately pervasive—irony of the novel invokes Ecclesiastes. Thus, Max Ashkenazi, trapped in St. Petersburg by the Bolshevik Revolution, laments:

> He was a superfluous being in this huge city. He was superfluous and naked. His houses had been seized, his money in the banks sealed up, his stocks and bonds

completely devaluated. No, he said to himself, there are
no eternal things. Even houses and factories are not
eternal things. He had thought to prepare himself
against the worst by putting his money into solid, tangible possessions. Now they were all gone.

When Max finally dies, his factory is in receivership,
his son has fled to Paris, and Lodz is a dying city.

With this shift in tone, form and theme fuse forcefully and effectively, allowing us to see that *The
Brothers Ashkenazi* is thematically and structurally
patterned as an illustration of the truth of *Ecclesiastes*. Repeatedly the narrative configurations of the
novel trace Max's struggle upward to an apex of
achievement, only to reverse his fortunes when success
seems to be in his grasp. The images of regal splendor
and of female seductiveness that Baron von Heidel-
Heidellau and Gertrude Ashkenazi see when they look
in the mirror are other instances of the novel's organized representation of human folly. The cool irony of
the enlightened skeptic, with which the novel opens,
gives way by the conclusion to the profound wisdom
of the Hebraic ironist. I. J. Singer has not strayed as
far from his father's court as he might have
thought.

*The Brothers Ashkenazi* does not follow the usual
demography of the Yiddish familial epic from patriar-
chal unity to progenitive dispersal, yet it continues to
order its material in mythic patterns that ultimately
affect its form as profoundly as do its parallels to
actual history. In addition to the correspondences
with Ecclesiastes, there is as a dominant pattern the
primordial struggle of brother against brother. Like
Cain and Abel, or Jacob and Essau, Max and Jacob
Ashkenazi feud for the favor of father, wife, community, and God. Corollaries of this archetype are the
mythic dissonances of son versus father and daughter

versus mother. I. J. Singer searches the entanglements of these relationships with great ordering skill and sense of biblical tonality. What one generation splits asunder, another joins together. Max displaces his father as agent for the Huntze factory and in the process alienates his brother. His daughter Gertrude, however, marries her uncle, requiting in the act her mother's love for Jacob. Through that marriage, Jacob the hated brother becomes the estranged son-in-law, who in ironic reverse of the biblical parable, eventually welcomes home Max the prodigal brother / father-in-law, who has wasted his heritage of life in endless getting and keeping. Like a leitmotif, growth and consolidation, conflict and disruption, characterize both the generations of the Ashkenazis and the life cycle of the Lodz textile industry.

Isaac Bashevis is less conventional than his brother in his search for a literary form that is paradigmatic of history. The meaningful pattern that *The Family Moskat* imposes on human experience is less obtrusively epical than that of *The Brothers Ashkenazi*, simultaneously more concerned with "real life" in its ordering of literary effects and yet more uncompromising in its insistence on what Louis D. Rubin, Jr., in *The Curious Death of the Novel*, has called the validity of the novel's own representation. To achieve such a union of paradoxes demands a sensibility of immense subtlety and invention—of endless deviousness which rigorously resists the temptation of relaxing into manner.

Like *The Brothers Ashkenazi*, *The Family Moskat* ties the fortunes of a family to the history of a city: the Warsaw ghetto. Unlike *The Brothers Ashkenazi* it does not chronicle the genesis and apocalypse of this family as a neat parabola with a beginning, middle, and end. It ignores first cause. Human events link in

an endless chain of this and then that, without de-
monstrable origin or clean-cut conclusion. To treat
fictionally of one or of several events is merely to
separate an instant from the persistent sequence of
time. This, in effect, Isaac Bashevis implies by the
confines of his novel, which are less limits than arbi-
trary starts and stops, starting with the eighty-year-old
patriarch Meshulam Moskat's senseless third marriage
and stopping with Asa Heshel Bannet's perverse wel-
come of the Nazi. Climaxes are denied, flattened out,
buried in a multiplicity of corollary details and incidents: Hadassah's stirring elopement with Asa Heshel
and her ignominious return become simply incidents
told in conjunction with the no less important dramas
of Meshulam's death and the agent Koppel's robbery
of the Moskat safe; her and Asa's love is adulterously
consummated as an understated anticlimax to the circumstances of the mismatched marriage of each to
another person. Not the actual family of the Moskats
(Meshulam and his four sons and three daughters)
but Abram Shapiro, Koppel Berman, and Asa Heshel
—all linked to the Moskats by marriage—figure most
extensively in the novel. This curious indirection of
the narrative, which focuses on non-Moskats, supports
the novel's resistance to climaxes. Not one theme but
a phalanx of complementary motifs are developed:
the divisive consequences of the Enlightenment, of
the secularization of the Jews, and of the deterioration
of their sense of spiritual destiny into a hankering
after occultism; the young man up from the provinces,
as symptomatic of the break up of the *shtetl* and the
ghetto way of life, and of the atrophy of Chassidic joy
and energy; the *fin de siècle* nihilism of a culture bent
on self-destruction, on inversion of the redemptive
hope for everlasting life into the secular suspicion that
death equals the truth about life. Interestingly, the

narrative becomes more episodic as it plunges toward the final dissolution of Moskats, Polish Jews, and European society in the holocaust of the Second World War—the structure of the novel corresponding increasingly to the passing of a sense of family unity with the death of Meshulam and to the loss of cultural cohesion with the advance of the twentieth century. By such indirect means Isaac Bashevis suggests both the decline of a family and the disintegration of a society, and approximates structurally and thematically the unclimactic flow of time.

But Isaac Bashevis's imagination has an ordering as well as an historical instinct. Probably more than anyone writing fiction in America today, he has mastered the skill of arranging his narrative so that its details and actions reverberate with symbolic overtones. A dominant leitmotif in *The Family Moskat* is death, underscored by such subtle details as the date on which the story opens: the year of the sinking of the *Titanic*. It is also the eve of the assassination at Sarajevo. At the outset two generations of the Moskats are already old, almost finished with living. Hence the emphasis of the novel, its tone, is on the end of things rather than on their beginnings, the mood Chekhovian. The moribundity of the Moskats foreshadows the passing of old-fashioned Chassidism. The opening on Reb Meshulam's octogenarian marriage to a widow past the age of conception is ironically linked in its reference to sterility with the closing on Asa Heshel's obsessive refusal to flee doomed Warsaw, preferring instead to wander through the city bidding his family and his old friends good-bye. The time of the year seems always to be winter. Snow is forever falling. Asa Heshel and Hadassah meet as the first snow of the season falls. They disclose their love for each other during another snowfall. The mood is developed in

Asa Heshel's disgust at bringing new life into being; his forcing his first wife Adele to have two abortions; Abram Shapiro's barren affair with Ida; and Koppel and Leah's consumation of their twenty-year love in marriage after she is finished with child bearing.

Singer has organized his fictional version of a culture's death agonies according to the special antithesis of old and new that characterizes the transition of the East European ghetto Jew from sidelocks, caftan, and Talmudic study to shaven face, Western dress, and scientific skepticism. "Willingly or unwillingly," he has commented about *The Family Moskat*, "we have enacted here the struggle between two generations—the old and the new—religious Judaism and the secular." This dualistic conception of his story sets up a thematic discord with the otherwise conventional three-generation structure of the story—which indicates his daring willingness to adapt the Yiddish family chronicle to his unique artistic vision. Hence his relative disregard of the second generation of Moskats, in favor of the first and third, and his inventive solution of the resultant plotting problem by concentration of his attention on non-Moskats. The focus of the narrative on Asa Heshel, Abram Shapiro, and Koppel Berman results in a structural duality that simultaneously emphasizes the Moskats and the non-Moskats, the old and the new, the orthodox and the libertine—in which stasis, neither movement backward nor forward, is the keynote. In keeping with their *Weltschmerz*, the Warsaw Jews are depicted as occupying the dead center of change. The enlightened Jew—the new Jew—has "lost the initiative," so Hertz Yanovar tells the Polish police. "We are powerless not only in relation to the Christians, but to our own brethren as well." The symbolic action of the narrative depicts the Judaic and the secular as existing side by side, irrevocably alienated from each other. The point is quietly made when we are told that on the evening of Reb Meshulam's first day home after his pointless third marriage to a non-Chassid there came from the salon "the sound of rumbling bass notes on the piano, like distant thunder, as Adele [his modernized step-daughter] ran her fingers over the keys," and "From elsewhere in the flat came the voice of Meshulam Moskat chanting in his study, his tones deep and resonant." The Warsaw Jew has worked himself into a cul-de-sac; he is at a standstill, unwilling to turn back to the assurance and piety of old, unable to move forward into a completely secular world. This dichotomy, underlining the point that the novel is concerned with documenting, is dramatized in the last scene between Asa Heshel and his mistress Barbara. With the Nazi expected momently, Asa the ex-Talmudic student opts for death. He elects to stay on in Warsaw. His mood is pessimistic. His gaze is on the past. Barbara the Marxist functionary opts for life. She determines to flee the city "to keep on fighting for a while." Her dogged optimism, secular and socialistic, refuses to believe that the outcome of Armageddon is yet decided.

Singer is, of course, always the novelist, concerned with developing characters and telling a story. His intense awareness of the ambiguity of human experience precludes the hardening of these ingredients into allegory. Thus, my ostensible identification of both Reb Meshulam and Asa Heshel with the godly past oversimplifies the symbolic action I have been outlining. If Meshulam and Asa are physically similar, both tall and thin, they yet embody ironic reversals of one another's appearances and habits of mind, at least when first introduced to us. Meshulam dresses like a Westerner but thinks like an orthodox Jew. Asa is garbed like a pious Chassid but is already bitten with the skeptical ideas of the Enlightenment. Meshulam speaks Polish and Russian, as well as Yiddish; and his third marriage, death, and funeral are travesties of lust and greed. Asa quickly shaves his beard, cuts his earlocks (the routine with the barber is repeated in the final scene), and discards his caftan, but he never succeeds wholly in emancipating himself from the idealism of his Talmudic days. Adele, his first wife, perceives this fact about Asa years after their divorce:

> She had never been able to understand what it was that tortured him . . . but suddenly she knew: he was not a worldly man by his very essence. He was one of those who must serve God or die. He had forsaken God, and because of this he was dead—a living body with a dead soul. She was astonished that this simple truth had eluded her until now.

This confusion of appearance and reality pervades the novel. Its thematic importance is such that a mirror metaphor—one of the most complex of the controlling metaphors of the novel—everywhere reinforces it. The image, of course, strikes at the roots of the narcissism of the Moskats; but more thematically it defines the degree to which the person in the mirror has altered in appearance. Thus Asa Heshel confronts himself in a restaurant mirror on his first day in Warsaw: "Suddenly a figure materialized in front of him, horrifyingly familiar and at the same time puzzlingly strange. It was his own face, his own features he was seeing in a mirror nearby." The significant clue to this momentary hallucination, we learn a sentence later, is that "he had shaved his face clean" the night before. Asa Heshel, the promising *cheder* boy up from the country *shtetl* of Tereshpol Minor less than twenty-four hours, is already metamorphosing into the

Westernized Jew. In its most profound sense, the mirror image measures the departure of the Warsaw Jew, as represented by the Moskat family, from traditional Judaic ways. In effect the image in the mirror reminds its viewer of his loss of true identity. Significantly, this vision of one's *Doppelgänger* is experienced by those—Asa Heshel, Hadassah, Koppel, Abram Shapiro, and Masha—who have strayed farthest from their origins.

The alarming actuality of this transformation lies in its irreversibility. These lost souls find to their horror that the wraith of their past existence is equally foreign to them, that they cannot return to a "pre-Adamic" life. Thus, when Asa Heshel visits Tereshpol Minor with his wife Adele, he resumes for appearance's sake the outward semblance of a Chassid. But when Adele brings him a hand mirror so that he might look at himself, "he hardly recognized his own face; the sprouting beard on his chin and cheeks and the traditional skullcap on his head had taken away the last bit of his resemblance to the Westerner." Similarly, Hadassah describes in her diary the preparations for her orthodox wedding to the pious Fishel Kutner: "They've taken my measurements for a matron's wig. I tried it on and in the mirror I hardly recognized myself. With all of the tragedy, I really wanted to burst out laughing. Well, I'll wear it, just as though it were my cross." Notice Hadassah's confusion of two sets of religious views as well as ultimately two cultures in her association of *matron's wig* with *cross*! Three weeks later, now married to a man she loathes, she writes in her girlhood diary, "I am sitting at a writing-desk, a matron's wig on my head, and my own face is as strange to me as my soul. I have gone through all of it: the ritual bath, the wedding ceremony, and all the rest. I will confide no more of my

secrets to you, my diary. You are pure; I am unclean."
For Hadassah the road back to orthodoxy by way of
the ritual bath has ironically led her only to new
uncleanliness.

The full implications of this appearance / reality
motif—the reduction of meaningful religio-communal
solidarity to its obscene contrary—is masterfully depicted in the giggling, sweating, drunken mob attend-
ing the Channukah masked ball. Hadassah watches
with stunned eyes as a "bewildering variety of masked
figures went by: Russian generals with epaulets, Polish
grandees in elegant caftans, Germans in spiked hel-
mets, rabbis in fur hats, yeshivah students in velvet
skullcaps; sidelocks dangling below their ears." It is
some time before she realizes that these are "merely
masquerade costumes." With inobtrusive symbolic
power, the Channukah ball concentrates for us the
radical nature of the alienation of a people from the
traditional patterns that once gave significance to
their lives. Person and *Doppelgänger* have merged in
the Warsaw Jews' impious parody of their old selves.
Costumed in the garb of a lost idealism, reminders of
the unfulfilled aspirations of earlier years, they have
become an empty approximation of their original
identities. Ironically they even ape the gentiles who
will eliminate eventually their need for graves in the
ovens of Auschwitz.

This loss of spiritual as well as personal identity is
approximately enough everywhere in the novel associated with death. Thus, Masha the apostate, who has
married a Pole and converted to Christianity, looks at
herself in a bureau mirror after the all-night Channukah ball: "Her face was deathly pale. Her hair, which
she had had so carefully dressed the day before, was
now disheveled. There were rings under her eyes. 'My
God, they bury better-looking carcasses than me,'

Masha thought, remembering a favorite phrase of her mother's." Similarly, Koppel, who has emigrated to America, visits Warsaw only to see "someone profoundly familiar and yet equally strange" come toward him as he walks into the lobby of the hotel. "It was himself, Koppel, his own image reflected in a mirror. The face was yellow, the hair at the temples almost gray." Masha and Koppel—as well as the libertine Abram Shapiro and the atheist Asa Heshel—stare, like Dorian Gray, at the scabrous image of their inner being. Singer could easily have entitled his novel The Fall of the House of Moskat.

History is arrested for these people, even as they grow old and paradoxically rush toward their final *dénouement* in the Nazi concentration camps. Thus, the aging Abram Shapiro ends the Channukah ball in meaningless copulation with a former servant girl of the Moskats, amid the sordid paraphernalia of a kitchen. This effort to reassure himself that he is alive ironically brings on a heart attack. Singer directs us to the significance of the scene when he has Abram drop his watch. The slut picks it up and holds it to her ear. "Did it stop?" Abram asks. "Yes," she answers. "Ah," he muses, "Yes, it was an omen. He was dying. In five-and-thirty years the watch had never stopped. He closed his eyes." Abram does not die this time. But Singer's point is clear: bankruptcy of cultural values removes a people from the stream of time. They can only eddy in the physical activity of a pointless present. "Was it possible that past time had no being," Asa Heshel asks himself, when he learns of his wife Hadassah's death by a German bomb and he is unable to weep one tear for her. In a terrifyingly real Kantian sense, time has become illusory for him. It is appropriate that time—or more accurately non-time—obsesses Asa Heshel, who has most determinedly cut himself free of his Hebraic roots, and that eternity, which encompasses a true sense of all time, should be identified in his mind with the heavy odor of the synagogue, "compounded of candle wax, dust, fast days, and eternity." This stress on arrested time neatly qualifies the forward sweep of history traditionally chronicled in the Yiddish familial novel. It supports metaphysically the fictional statement of the dualistic structure, the mirror metaphor, and the appearance / reality motif, that the Warsaw Jews can neither move with nor reverse history.

I am indebted to Sidney Adler for pointing out to me that Singer decided in the English translation of *The Family Moskat* to end with the next-to-last chapter of the original Yiddish version. In the final chapter, in the Yiddish, he depicts the state of mind of the characters during the early hours of the Nazi invasion of Poland. The pious Jews examine and reaffirm their faith in the Judaic values which have long sustained them, while the secularized Jews discover the shortcomings of the ideals that they have harkened after. As bombs fall, Asa Heshel, Nyunie Moskat, and Masha all turn back to the spiritual sustenance of the Old Testament. Thus the Yiddish conclusion celebrates in elevated tone the immemorial faith of the Jews in the final spiritual redemption of man. The English version refuses to follow this Yiddish tradition of the didactic—and rightly so, for the ambiguous note of the English ending not only poses for one last time the thematic dualism of the story, here as represented by Asa Heshel and Barbara Fishelson, but in its openness, or incompleteness, also reiterates structurally the temporal motif that man's journey to the end of time, as the lesson of history reminds us, remains for his generation ever unfinished.

Isaac Bashevis shows more audacious originality

than his brother Israel Joshua in fitting the Yiddish family chronicle to his vision of human experience. He dares to eliminate the epic vein that *The Brothers Ashkenazi* still adheres to. As in Greek tragedy he syncopates the sweep of generations into a final doomed year or two, without sacrificing Tolstoian breadth of canvas. The effect of *The Family Moskat* is that of a camera winging panoramically across the gulf if time and place, while simultaneously zooming down for intimate close-ups. Nowhere is control of his material more dramatically illustrated than in Isaac Bashevis' choice of Asa Heshel as the lens through which much of the action is refracted. Asa Heshel is spiritually paralyzed and intellectually bankrupt. Hence his vision can only be unheroic and fragmentary. I. J. Singer's selection of Max Ashkenazi as his vantage point dictates, contrariwise, that the narrative have a certain *élan*, given Max's ambitions, an heroic drive toward grand goals. The dramatic rightness of each novelist's sensitivity to the tonal nuances demanded of his material appears comparable, for example, in his portrait of a roué. Although a potential wastrel, Jacob Ashkenazi eventually performs in heroic fashion. It is stylistically, as well as thematically, fitting that his butterfly existence not be rendered dramatically then but rather alluded to secondhand by his biased brother Max. Abram Shapiro, however, acts out his compromised existence without narrative intermediary, the symbolic action of his deterioration ultimately representative of the fate of a people. Similarly, time eats at the entrails of both Max Ashkenazi and Asa Heshel; but only for Asa is its daily horror fortified, not transcended, by the form of the novel.

Both Singers reveal an excruciating time-sense. Both find the Yiddish familial epic irresistible but its fixed form limiting. Each in his idiosyncratic way attempts to order his materials into a fictional construct attentive to the demands of history. Both *The Brothers Ashkenazi* and *The Family Moskat* manage to be at once thematically consistent to their own versions of reality, and yet cognizant of the linear endlessness of time.

# Conjuring Reality
## I. B. Singer's *The Magician of Lublin*

CYRENA N. PONDROM

Isaac B. Singer in *The Magician of Lublin* is a con-
jurer who turns his magic to the creation of a vision of
a forty-year-old man's crisis of conscience. In his novel
—very probably his best—the reader who escapes the
power of the storytelling for a moment in order to
reflect can discern three separate patterns of meaning.
There is first the tale of a man who rejects his past life
and turns to penitence. Here, in the literal world of
the novel, Singer accomplishes both the vivid realization of an individual character's struggles and the
representation of recurrent (perhaps mythic or archetypal) human experiences. Then, around the uncom-
plicated certainties of literal plot or archetypal situation Singer weaves an examination of the uncertainties of ethical behavior, and here he constructs a
moral world that is insolubly ambivalent. And finally,
using all the concreteness of his detailed and almost
tangible fictional world, Singer turns to metaphysical
themes. Thus at the last he forces the reader to revise
his understanding both of literal fact and moral
choice in the novel, for he suggests that "facts" have
only the meanings they are assigned by human beings,
that man may be a "magician" indeed.

Yasha Mazur, the magician, leaves his pious, faithful wife, Esther, in Lublin to go on a show tour to

93

Warsaw. As he goes he picks up Magda, his mistress and assistant, and tells Zeftel, another mistress, to look him up in Warsaw. All the while he debates whether or not he can bring himself to "convert a little" in order to marry Emilia, the Gentile professor's widow with whom he is infatuated, and to commit a theft to finance the elopement. He attempts the theft and fails, receiving in the effort the foot injury which precludes his magic performance. Emilia casts him off, and he immediately finds Magda a suicide and Zeftel in bed with a pimp. Deeply shaken, he re-evaluates his entire past life as dishonest and sinful, and returns to Esther's care in Lublin, where he bricks himself into a cell in his backyard and devotes himself to pious meditation.

Much of the emphasis in these events lies in examination of what happens to an individual in crisis when he is not supported by conventional cultural forms. It is a theme to which Singer has returned again and again in novels from *Satan in Goray* to *The Manor*. But when we ask if the literal should be seen as symbolic we observe that the tale invites our memory of some important analogues. In one sense the book is a parallel to the biblical account of Jacob wrestling with the angel. Yasha feels the presence of a dybbuk as he tries to steal, injures his leg like Jacob during the theft episode, and at the end is even called Reb Jacob the Penitent. The pattern common to the two stories is the archetype of the test. A man, basically not evil, is confronted with a moral or spiritual challenge which after much suffering and through both his own choices and the grace of God he survives, perhaps triumphantly. Some basic features of the Odysseus myth are also relevant: a hero journeys out through much vicissitude and returns finally to reclaim his home, his identity and his faithful wife. Correspond-ingly, Yasha's crisis occurs during his trip to Warsaw and is precipitated by his romance with a Gentile woman; and his wife, Esther, bears the name of the Hebrew queen who saved her people from a gentile plot to exterminate them. From another standpoint, Yasha reenacts the historical myth of a chosen people who repeatedly turn away from God at the cost of terrible suffering, but who are preserved through the Covenant until they return to the Law. For all her irony, Emilia exclaims to Yasha as he confesses his attempted theft, "You must have some sort of covenant with God since he punished you directly on the spot." And in the introspective hallucinations which accompany Yasha's emotional upheaval following Magda's suicide one can even see the archetype of descent into the darkness of the self and, finally, a return to the light.

At this literal level it is the *type* of actions which occur (i.e., the pattern of test and resolution), not the *content* of the faith affirmed, which is significant. The novel is not the story of conversion from doubt to faith, nor from one kind of faith to another. At first and last Yasha holds a somewhat pantheistic view of a God who reveals himself in nature but not directly to prophets. One of the first descriptions of the man indicates these views: "When he was in the tavern, Yasha played the atheist but, actually, he believed in God. God's hand was evident everywhere. Each fruit, blossom, pebble, and grain of sand proclaimed Him." At the end of the book, Reb Jacob the Penitent rises in his brick prison, contemplates the snow on the sill of his only window, and meditates, "What can one call this force, if not God? . . . And what difference does it make if it's called nature? . . . He had sought a sign, yet every minute, every second, within him and outside, God signaled his presence." Significantly, the theological conceptions are identical in their stress on the manifestation of God in nature. And, furthermore, there is little change in the way in which faith is held, for even the penitent continues to be plagued by doubt.

Consequently, though we must recognize the symbolic and archetypal importance of Yasha's actions, we may not treat the novel as a simple linear development, showing a "necessary choice" of "total faith," as J. S. Wolkenfeld has claimed in an article in *Criticism* in 1962. However, while faith does not change in the novel, action does. Yasha adopts the ritual of prescribed religious practice and attempts to avoid situations in which he may sin. Does he then achieve "the good life" and may the novel be seen as a rejection of evil and choice of the good? The answer is no, and we must exculpate Singer from the charge of the sentimentally easy resolution to the narrative which Max Schulz has charged him with in a 1967 Modern Language Association meeting paper. The ironic conclusion prevents sentimentality. There is no simple return to home and right action, for an ironic context makes the absolute ethical value of Yasha's acts ambivalent.

In fact, exploring the ambivalence of the ethical meaning of human acts is one of the chief concerns of the novel. Singer uses the background of an Orthodox society in which a code of conduct is prescribed down to the last detail, but until the "Epilogue" moral choices are presented through the eyes of Yasha the skeptic. The descriptive background and the narrative view thus offer the two antithetical moral perspectives that operate in the book: they may be called the absolute and the relative, the simplistic and the sophisticated, or the profound and the sophistic, depending on the critic's outlook. On the one hand is the traditional view that good and evil are clearly defined and divinely revealed, and that the individual must choose one or the other; archetypal interpretation presumes this simplicity. On the other hand is the "modern" skeptic, or agnostic view that good and evil are not always dissociated and may even be arbitrarily defined by man; ethical and metaphysical interpretations of the novel lead to this view.

There really is no mediation between the views; either Yasha is a holy man as a penitent or he is just a man like all others, equally involved in evil. He believes, of course (when he is not overwhelmed by doubt), that he has been transformed and that as a penitent he is shielded from sin. The last sentence before the "Epilogue" records: "And even as he stood there staring, he knew he was undergoing some sort of transformation, that he would never again be the Yasha he had been. . . . He had seen the hand of God. He had reached the end of the road." But from a skeptic's position the change is more in form than in content. As a magician, he performs tricks that bring him regard as "sorcerer" and wonder worker. When he turns penitent, Yasha finds himself acting as another kind of magician:

> Men and women began to visit him as though he were a thaumaturgic rabbi. They sought his advice, begged him to intercede on their behalf. . . . Before long there was talk in the city of the miracles performed by Yasha the Penitent. He only had to make a wish, it was rumoured, and the sick grew well.

He acknowledges the limits of his thaumaturgic skills, as he had insisted there was no "magic" in his tricks, but in both cases he permits people to believe he exercises power beyond the natural.

Despite his good intentions, he also continues to

injure others in his role as penitent. A deserted wife, unsatisfied at Yasha's responses, has to be dragged away as she shouts at him, "Scum, whoremaster, murderer!" Her language is almost identical with that hurled at him by his mistress Magda, only hours before she hangs herself in despair at his impending desertion. Moreover, his faithful Esther is far more injured by his penitence than by his earlier affairs. During his brief stay at home at the first of the book, Esther muses, "Why did she love him? She knew he led a wicked life . . . but she preferred him above any man, no matter how exalted—even a rabbi." She is constant in her preferences. When Yasha chides during the construction of his cell, "Why all this wailing? I'm not dead yet," she responds, "If only you were." Thus she becomes in his penitence the deserted wife she never was throughout his many affairs.

First and last, for Yasha, the fundamental values are a reverence for life and personal integrity, and the basic ethical questions for him, whether he can avoid injuring others and be honest both to others and to himself; or in one application of a chief symbol, whether or not he can walk the tightrope. Consequently, the interpretation that he continues both to deceive and to injure is a fundamental contradiction of his view of the meaning of his transformation. Such an interpretation, of course, is from the skeptic's perspective. From the standpoint of faith, the penitent's "miracles" would be no deception, and the burden on his wife her *mitzvah*. The contradiction is so fundamental that even the description of the book's structure must change with the moral perspective being used. From the viewpoint of the traditional or absolute view, the book builds up to a crucial encounter with moral reality—the theft that fails and the loss of three women—and then continues linearly in the

*dénoument* of justified penitence. From the relativis-
tic standpoint, the book is a cycle: a period of moral
ambiguity, a traumatic encounter with "black and
white" ethical issues, and a return to moral ambiguity.
Thus the ethical meaning of Yasha's penitence is literally ambivalent: it is subject to alternate and irrecon-
cilable interpretations.

It is also ambivalent in another way. Even if Yasha
does continue to deceive and fail to recognize the way
his penitence injures, his actions in the epilogue bring
good as well. His failings, Singer shows, result not
from a variety of evil peculiar to him, but from the
elusiveness of the ideal of honesty and from the
human condition itself.

One of the first and most persistent challenges to
Yasha's honest action is the ethical paradox that one
can deceive while telling the truth. When his friend
Schmul praises the sword act and calls him a "master
of deception," Yasha protests, "I don't deceive anyone." Schmul, however, wants to be deceived; he will
not believe that Yasha really swallows the sword.
"You big simpleton," the magician replies, "how can
anyone deceive the eye? You happen to hear the word
'deception' and you keep repeating it like a parrot. Do
you have any idea what the word means?"

But Yasha has an inadequate idea of the meaning
of "deception" too, for he is here treating honesty as a
matter of legal technicality. He has, presumably,
learned to swallow the sword without injury. Thus he
muses about Schmul and his kind. "They see with
their own eyes but they don't believe." But he depends on their disbelief for the effectiveness of his act.
He counts on their preference for illusion, for
"magic," when he literally swallows the sword. Thus,
paradoxically, he accomplishes his deception by the
most straightforward openness. (The same perception

of the paradoxical nature of "honesty" appears in Kierkegaard's demonic merman in *Fear and Trembling,* in the spiteful confession of Dostoevsky's underground man, and in Clamance's ironic monologue in Camus's *The Fall.*) Consequently, Yasha is not what he claims and conceives himself to be; he deceives, but by a means that enables him to conceal the fact from himself.

Such paradoxical dishonesty is a prominent feature of Yasha's major relationships. The magician deceives himself in his affairs as he does concerning his magic act. He has carried on many affairs over the years, some of them semi-permanent, like the one with his assistant, Magda. But in all this, he says, "in some final sense his marriage had remained sacred to him. He had never concealed that he had a wife and he had always made it clear that he would do nothing that would jeopardize this relationship." But though he tells his mistresses he has a wife, his actions permit them to deceive themselves about his attitude to their relationship. He maintains an apartment with Magda in Warsaw, for example, and supports her family. Thus he treats his words as more significant than his actions and deceives himself when he rejects responsibility for Magda's dependence. Magda, at first, is as willing to be deceived as Schmul, and Yasha finds her illusion convenient and even comforting. But his romance with Emilia causes Magda to seek more open signs of reassurance. Under this pressure Yasha moves from complicity in Magda's self-deception towards open untruth. As he prepares to go to Emilia's house he assures Magda "that no matter what happened to him he would never forsake her."

Thus as the book proceeds Yasha becomes involved in steadily more overt deception. Yasha's assurances to Magda escape being completely false only because of

his own inner indecision and, ultimately, the collapse
of his plans. This development in personal relationships is accompanied by a similar evolution in what
we may call "business affairs." Yasha's dishonesty in-
creases from the subtle deception of Schmul as part of
his act to the attempted burglary of the miser's house.
He flees when he is unable to open the safe, and
experiences his first wave of penitence and insight
while standing in a prayer shawl in the synagogue
which—ironically—he has entered to escape pursuit.

> He . . . was aghast at the extent of his degradation and,
> what was perhaps worse, his lack of insight. He had
> fretted and worried and ignored the very essence of the
> problem. He had reduced others to dirt and *did not
> see—pretended not to see*—how he himself kept sink-
> ing deeper in the mud. (Italics mine)

As he recognizes, his increasing dishonesty is partially the result of willful self-deception. But it is also
partially the result of a fundamental and apparently
inescapable lack of understanding of the motivations
of his own actions. Yasha often seems in the grip of
powerful drives he can no more control than he can
understand. He senses his attraction to Emilia's
daughter, Halina, and condemns it, but seems to regard his future actions on that matter as beyond his
control. More significant for his present imbroglio, he
has repeated dreams of power: visions of himself
flying anywhere with artificial wings, as a divine hyp-
notist, as emperor of the world, as a leader of the Jews
out of exile. In such a context his decision to do a
somersault on the tightrope, "a stunt as yet unat-
tempted by any other performer," seems the counter-
part of his efforts to dominate the affections of five
women simultaneously: not the unethical actions of a
dishonest man but the lust for power of a man who

cannot control his psychological drives. What is more, both his planned stunt and the increasingly dangerous complexity of his personal affairs fit meaningfully into yet another psychological pattern: that of a man whose sense of guilt or unworthiness compels him to seek ever more difficult circumstances until failure arrives to justify his guilt. Yasha wants what he tells the waiter: "To pay." His manager, Wolsky, suggests the same possibility after Yasha injures his foot: "I've seen how artists commit suicide. Scramble up the mountain for years but just when the summit is in view, fall and smash themselves. Why this should be I don't know. Perhaps they have a taste for the gutter." Since to be ethically significant "honest action" must imply the possibility of conscious choice, these symbolic images of flight and deliberate fall suggest that honesty and integrity may be rendered meaningless by the unconscious forces which mock attempts at ethical control. (A Sartrian rather than Freudian analysis of consciousness, of course, would treat "unconscious" forces as another example of self-deception.)

But there are other challenges to integrity that lie outside the confines of the mind of the hero. Sometimes, the text suggests, language itself seems to make honesty impossible. On the way to Warsaw with Magda Yasha engaged in a long meditation about his interest in Emilia. He wonders whether or not he can bring himself to theft in order to run away to Italy with her, and then remembers "he had always prided himself on his honesty." Here, precisely focussed on the question of theft, there is no problem with the word's meaning: it refers to a code of conduct, in which an honest man will not violate the Eighth Commandment. But the context quickly broadens. On the following page Yasha recognizes "he could not even be sure . . . whether the feeling he had is really what is known as love. Would he be able to remain true to her?" Moments later, Magda, riding beside him, asks about Emilia. He assures her "my love for you won't change" and pledges never to forget her, but "he did not know himself if he were telling the truth or lying." Now his use of the concept of honesty implies not just a code of conduct, but also a belief that Yasha can know himself and his own situation truthfully, and further, that his character and emotional states are consistent and predictable. Is he honest about his love for Magda only if his statement is an accurate prediction of his future conduct? (But then, what should the future conduct of one who "loves" be?) Or is he honest if his words accurately reflect his current feelings, even if they are reversed tomorrow? But what has he implied about his current feelings when he says he loves? Obviously, as he sees, the problem is not only with the referent of honesty but also of love. To Yasha, to be honest, with its echoes of law and logic, implies that he is not saying one thing and its opposite; this is, however, to treat love as an unambiguous term with a single meaning. In fact, implicit in ordinary usage is the conventional moral assumption that an *honest* statement of love means what it "ought" to mean: to wit, that he loves only Magda and that his love will be demonstrated by its conventional marital expression. But this moral definition of love is not a descriptive one, and here we encounter again the problem of absolute and logical conceptions in a relative and shifting world. Human personality, Singer shows, is the realm of paradox rather than logic, and the logical and orderly terms for human values sit loosely on the moving stream of personality, neither explaining nor defining. Thus deception and illusion in the novel turn on a linguistic and conceptual as well as an ethical problem. Not only may Yasha deceive by being truthful, but language itself, with moral precepts and abstract expectations smuggled into what seems empirical description, falsifies his experience as he tries to communicate it.

Confronted with ethical paradox and linguistic ambiguity, Yasha is also plagued with the problem of what he is that he should be faithful to. Or, in the stark terms that Emilia's young daughter uses, "What's a Jew?" Yasha has no doubts that he is a Jew because his parents were—but he is racked by uncertainty about whether he is denying his heritage unless he observes the conventional religious and cultural practices. Does integrity lie in expressing his being in conventional practice or in remaining faithful to his scepticism? At the first he is shown as separated from the traditional community: "Jews—an entire community of them—spoke to a God no one saw. . . . Yasha often envied their unswerving faith." He himself is "half Jew, half gentile—neither Jew nor gentile. He had worked out his own religion." The ambivalence of his attitudes is captured by the first of three occasions in which he seeks refuge in a synagogue. Caught in a rainstorm on the way to Warsaw, he drives into the synagogue courtyard and seeks protection in the study-house. It has been so long since he has been in a temple that all seems "strangely foreign to him, yet familiar." He experiences a sudden sense of continuity with his heritage: "He was part of this community. Its roots were his roots. He bore its mark upon his flesh." But he goes immediately to an inn where he poses as a Pole, because he is travelling with Magda, who is gentile. Torn by remorse, he sees the grandmother of the Jewish innkeeper as one "aware of a truth known only to those not deceived by the vanity of worldly things." Each of the next two trips to the synagogue results in a deeper encounter with traditional attitudes. He accepts the prayer shawl he refused at the previous synagogue when he seeks refuge in the Gnoyne Street temple after his attempted theft. There he stands penitent at his sin, shamed "because he had betrayed this fraternity," overcome with the return of childhood faith. He leaves with the vow "I must be a Jew! . . . A Jew like all the others!"

This vow is significant because it represents not a recognition of self-identity but the acceptance of moral obligation to act in a certain way. When Yasha leaves the synagogue "his earlier complaints about religion reasserted themselves." But his third trip to the synagogue on the following day ends with his resumption of the vow to submit to religious discipline—an intention made permanent by his immediate discovery of Magda's suicide. He now believes that "he had alienated himself from the pious but he had not gone over to the camp of the assimilated." And, "What did the assimilated Jews have? Nothing of their own." He renounces his contempt for "man-made dogmas" and concludes that they are necessary: "an abstract faith," he says, "invariably led to sin." Thus he leaves the synagogue determined to express his heritage by reconciling himself to the pious and becoming obedient—without compromise—to religious law.

But this is a decision to be true not to what he is as a man, but to a tradition. It is a decision to reduce multiplicity and ambiguity to simplicity, to cease trying to walk the tightrope. The extent to which this is a denial of his past personality is suggested by the words with which he plans (ironically, for she is really dead) to tell Magda of his vow: "Magda dear, I am dead. Take everything I own . . . and go home." Yasha has been "a maze of personalities—religious and heretical, good and evil, false and sincere." He has been a man of many gifts, an artist, intuitive, imitative, enigmatic, "not a normal person." His decision is a renunciation (as deception by worldly vanity) of his artistic gifts and his unrelenting honesty about religious faith. Thus even the action of violent repentance is ethically ambivalent: on the one hand it is a rejection of the evil he has wrought and an affirmation of his heritage, but on the other a denial of the reality of his complex and gifted personality. Thus challenged by the subtlety of "honesty," by self-deception, and by unconscious forces in his attempt to maintain his integrity as an honest man who values life above all, Yasha does not escape moral ambivalence even by the return to religious discipline, for in a complex world the very reduction to simplicity is a kind of falsification.

Still more significant for identifying the ethical meaning of Yasha's actions is the question of free will: to what extent is he free and hence responsible for what he does? Once again, the answer is ambivalent. Narration is chiefly through Yasha's eyes; consequently, narrated interpretation is not a reliable description of causes. Nonetheless, at the moment of all "decisions" Yasha alludes to something influencing him beyond his conscious awareness of alternatives. When he tells Emilia that he has decided to marry her, for example, the decision seems spontaneous: " 'I've come to you now and we won't be separated again!' he said, amazed at his own words. Until just now he had not yet made a decision."

Does he decide, and deceive himself about his responsibility for decision? Such is implied by his subsequent judgment that his past life has been sinful dishonesty. Or is he swept along by unconscious forces? Or, as he comes increasingly to feel, is his life governed by fate or non-temporal forces? Whether as a result of self-deception or not, Yasha's account of the episode of the theft is thick with references to unseen powers. Of the theft: "As long as it is inevitable, he said to himself, why not tonight? Evidently, it had been foreordained. How was it called?—predestination?" As he enters the miser's rooms: "The powers that control man's destiny had led him directly to Zaruski's hoard. . . . Unseen forces . . . ordered him to go into the bedroom." And after he has failed to open the safe: Yasha "knew . . . that the misfortune would not be confined to this night alone. That enemy which for years had lurked in ambush within him . . . had now gained the upper hand. Yasha felt its presence—a dybbuk, a satan, an implacable adversary who would disconcert him while he was juggling, push him from the tightrope, make him impotent."

Thus, at this point, a failure as a thief but not yet repentant, Yasha construes his actions to be the result of demonic possibilities within himself. After his repentance, he attributes his failure to the providence of an infinite God: "It was obvious that those in heaven did not intend to have him turn to crime, desert Esther, convert." From the perspective of repentance, random events seem necessary rather than contingent. In the synagogue for the third time, Yasha pulls a holy book from the shelf. It falls open at a passage on lust—"He closeth his eyes not to see evil"—and Yasha takes the text as a prescription for his own penitent action.

His expiation is a closing of his eyes to many of his possibilities. Is this a free selection of action (one way to walk the tightrope of being as ethical man) or flight from the realities of moral choice (a refusal to balance on the tightrope among conflicting ethical values)? The Lublin rabbi warns Yasha about the meaning of his actions: "The world had been created for the exercise of free will and the sons of Adam must constantly choose between good and evil. Why seal one's self in stone? The meaning of life was freedom and the abstinence from evil. Man deprived of free will was like a corpse." Nonetheless, Yasha finally wins the rabbi's blessing because of the purity of the intent of his action. There is, however, no final judgment on whether or not Yasha's choices are free. Thus the moral significance of his acts remains ambivalent because his degree of responsibility is subject to alternate interpretation.

And in addition, the intrinsic meaning of his expiation, as well as the extent of his freedom in choosing it, remains in question. As we have noted, the repetition of analogous metaphors suggests the irony that Reb Jacob the Penitent continues both to deceive and to injure, albeit in conscious commitment to faith. There is, as well, the possibility that Yasha's last actions are merely another expression of his lifetime inclination to play god. It is clear that Yasha was bitterly cruel to Magda; how much he may be implicated in her illusions concerning a possible life with him is not clear. After all, Magda is as free as he is to make a bargain and take the consequences. In fact, making himself responsible for her disaster may be just another form of illusion for Yasha—this time not an illusion of innocence but an arrogant assumption of too much guilt. Emilia suggests such a possibility in the ironic letter with which the book closes: "Reality is full of surprises. . . . The fact is you've committed no crime." He must not assume the guilt of other people's failure to bear their bargains; perhaps what he must do is impossible in this world. But such an insight escapes him. "Man can choose, after all," he thinks. "He sees everything if he chooses to see." But he does not reflect that his "honest" expiation of guilt is the harshest burden his wife has yet been forced to bear.

The possibility that Yasha at the end is playing god —a cosmic joke on others as well as himself—introduces the theme of metaphysical skepticism that undergirds the novel. This theme is developed metaphorically throughout the text. Yasha early exclaims, "Oh, God Almighty, You are the magician, not I! . . . To bring out plants, flowers and colors from a bit of black soil!" And Emilia's daughter reiterates the analogy: "God is mightier than you, Uncle Yasha. He can perform even finer tricks." The metaphor can serve to suggest that Yasha—seeking to control the lives of the women around him and treated as a prophet at the end—is guilty of hubris, that first and last he aspires to power beyond the condition of man. But it can also suggest that "God" is like Yasha, that the natural order of the universe is taken to be miraculous by people who, like Schmul, will not believe their eyes. From this perspective, it is the Yasha of the first pages who is undeceived about reality, and Reb Jacob the Penitent, smitten by life, who is the willing victim of illusion. The contrast is between interpretations of reality as temporal and as transcendental, between the views that human suffering is merely the inevitable result of natural processes and that it is religiously meaningful. In the symbolism of this novel, it is the choice between the interpretation that Yasha's suffering is punishment justified by covenant and, as he once claims, that it is the result of his own bungling.

Perhaps God does not exist, and it is the mind of man, not the mind of God, that conjures up the meaning of creation—and even the motion of creation. For Yasha the Magician is the creator, the artist, the inventor. It is his story, and the meanings he assigns to the events of his life contradict themselves

at beginning and end. He is the Icarus figure, determined to fly; overwhelmed by the tragedies to which
human beings are subject, he abandons the religion
that was his own invention and returns to the tested
ground of traditional faith. From this perspective,
Yasha's "transformation" in the horror of discovering
that "the faces of death and lechery . . . were the
same" is the transformation of exchanging our description of the universe for another, and the shift
from the spring imagery of the opening pages to the
snow of the last suggests the change is living death.
The revelation in his continual indecision is the shattering discovery that he is a potential thief rather than
an honest man if he so conceives himself: there are no
inviolable self-conceptions. Yet so much is man the
author of "reality" that if he believes himself an honest man he *cannot* open the safe—even though he has
many times before opened the same or a more compli-
cated lock. In fact, the responsibility for defining reality is so terrifying that he turns to religion, which
offers to define it for him. But recognition is there; in
an imaginary debate with the devil at the end he says:
"If there is no God, man must behave like God." He
sounds much like Ivan quoting Voltaire in *The Brothers Karamazov*: *"S'il n'existait pas Dieu, il faudrait
l'inventer*. And man has actually invented God."

Whether Yasha has invented God for himself neither he nor the reader can know. Is he an Icarus who
flies too near the sun, but who, nevertheless, prepares
the way for men who will fly? Or a Raskolnikov who
tries to "step beyond" conventional morality and is
relentlessly shown that there is a God? Unlike *Crime
and Punishment*, the "Epilogue" to *The Magician of
Lublin* does not stand outside the metaphysical questioning of the text, offering a perspective from which
to judge foregoing events. The skepticism is funda-

mental; it provides the context for the ambivalence of ethical meanings and the paradoxical contrast with the linear (and profound) simplicity of the literal and archetypal meanings. While the entire structure is undercut by the possibility that there is no God, that the "truth" of the meanings is that they are Yasha's (and ultimately, the novelist's) creation, the power of the symbolic pattern of test and redemption insists that throughout the text we take seriously the absolute and traditional interpretations of meaning. It is a paradoxical view. The "true," ritual world of the literal text and the radical skepticism of the metaphysical theme contradict each other, and the deepest statement of the book emerges from that conflict. In short, the paradox of the human situation is that man must live his individual life as if all he sees is objectively real, in a world in which ultimately all meanings may be the progeny of the creative mind of man. Because they represent the patterns of generations of human experience, there is meaning—truth—in Yasha's actions, even *if* they refer to a conception of reality which is untrue. Or as Singer himself has mused, "What is the truth of an account of psychic events? At least, the truth that someone thought them." Such a view could immerse the men of Singer's world, not in an amoral universe, but in a world of total responsibility: perhaps all men are magicians, who conjure the reality they see.

# Jacob Reborn, Zion Regained
## I. B. Singer's *The Slave*

FREDERICK R. KARL

> Two Souls, alas! reside within my breast,
> And each withdraws from, and repels, its brother.
> One with tenacious organs holds in love
> And clinging lust the world in its embraces;
> The other strongly sweeps, this dust above,
> Into the high ancestral spaces.

The atmosphere of Goethe's *Faust* would seem quite distant from the milieu of Singer's post-Chmelnicki Poland. *Faust* appears to be the embodiment of an entire culture as it faces both past and future. The mind of Faust, first scholarly, later searching and sensual, is the mind of Europe caught between enlightenment hierarchies and industrial dispersion, between pastoral placidity and urban anxiety, between class obeisance and individual enterprise. What possible relationship can it have with Singer's tortured seventeenth-century Jews who enjoy freedom only to the extent that their ghetto has remained unpenetrated by invading Cossack armies or vengeful Poles?

It is here, in this ambiguous area of freedom and bondage, that *The Slave* takes on significance, here that the moral issues indigenous to Singer's fiction begin to work themselves out. The protagonist, Jacob, is more firmly wrought, possibly, than any other of Singer's characters, and the contemporary reader, with few or no commitments to the intense religiosity of Jacob's feelings, can be engaged.

The reaction of the uncommitted reader, incidentally, is of considerable importance: that is, the whole question of how cogently Singer confronts a serious mind which is skeptical of many or most of the values he obviously takes seriously. Is he compelling only to those who have staked him out because of their own religious and professional affiliations, or those who edit Yiddish anthologies and build careers on interpreting unassimilated Jewish writers to assimilated Jewish readers? This is always a touchy point, because like most other primates, critics rarely admit their motives.

*The Slave* can allay many of these fears, although the unaffiliated reader may still find its Zionist conclusions contrived and stagey. But in its early and best parts, even though it is set three hundred years ago and might easily fall into the category of historical fiction, the novel captures the essence of modernity. That is, in the paradoxical nature of man's existence, given slavery, Jacob seeks freedom; gaining freedom, he finds slavery.

The substance of the situation is the substance of the European experience. As evidently as the desires of Faust are founded on the tensions between accomplishments and appetites, so the desires of Singer's characters—both protagonists and villains—strain first toward spirit and then toward flesh. A novel like *The Slave* is structured on a series of such conflicts, based on temptation and resistance, on what is natural, what unnatural, on that which is fleshly appetite and that which is spiritual striving, on what is man's and what is God's. Nature itself, the usual agent of spiritual resurrection, is opposed to the body, which festers and sores.

Even the minor characters play out various hierarchies of temptation. In the nobleman Adam Pilitzky, Singer sees a dying order that tries to hold on
through alternating excess and sorrow, with resultant
ennui and impotence. Even the name, Adam, becomes ironic, given Pilitzky's conflicting desires: the
first man becomes the least and last nobleman. His
wife, Lady Pilitzky, is consumed by sensual desires,
and yet recognizes the destruction rushing toward her
—symbolic of Poland, perhaps, and ominous for all
Jews who will remain. In another sector, the boatman
Waclaw (who like Charon ferries the shades of the
dead) turns out to be a follower of Sabbatai Zvi, the
false Messiah who converted to Mohammedanism—
the ultimate in temptation, conflict, and mismatched
ideas.

Although it has only rarely lent itself to American
fiction, the Faustian conflict is at home in the European mentality. Whereas the American can jump into
new life through the leaps of industry and opportunity, the European, accustomed to the slow tempi of
medieval economics and societies, must more readily
sacrifice his past for exotic desires. In older societies—
as in ghettoes—that grow only by tortured accretion,
change is not an obvious commodity; to involve oneself with it means a long and intricate play of forces.
Faustain soul-searching, therefore, is most meaningful
in those societies in which history results from disas-
ters like Chmelnicki's pogroms and their periodical
equivalent. If the social ethic, however, is itself built
on change, then the static becomes immoral. Nearly
any evil can be so justified if motivated by the need to
modify or develop. In a contrary society, in which
prayer is one's chief hope, Faust's willingness to sell
his soul takes on the quality of Jesus' temptation in
the wilderness, or, more moderately, Jacob's in the
gardens of Laban.

Jacob's Jewishness comes to him chiefly in the shape of suffering—for his family wiped out in the Cossack invasion, for his own exile and submerged identity, ultimately for the direction his appetites are taking him. Loosely working out the fate of his ancient ancestor in *his* pursuit of Rachel, Singer's Jacob finds, characteristically, that in realizing his object, he has embraced suffering and approached damnation.

The attractions of diverse situations, with the concurrent possibility of finding oneself in Gehenna, are essential to the Faustian theme. Singer, however, intensifies the consequences of choice, so that even when one is embracing what is desirable, the loved object has already turned into a witch, a reversal of the usual mythical procedure whereby love transmutes ugliness into beauty. Even the prospect of satisfaction brings no joy. Yasha the magician, Dr. Fischelson ("The Spinoza of Market Street"), the bailiff Koppel (*The Family Moskat*), Jacob obviously—all, regardless of station, experience pre-coital sadness. Most explicitly, in *The Manor*, Calman marries Clara out of lust, and yet on his wedding night, he "was ashamed to undress before so grand a lady. . . . He closed his eyes. Lust for Clara had faded away, and only fear remained."

As soon as man is torn by various appetites, as Faust, as Hawthorne's night creatures, as Dostoevsky's Ivan and Raskolnikov, he is an exile—to himself, to others, to the universe. Often the split is between Apollo and Dionysus, intellect and body. The image is of the saint torn by fleshly desires, the son wounded by his father and wishing his destruction, the peaceful citizen filled with a hunger for murder and massacre. It is also of the Jew attracted to a Gentile girl—the ultimate in the forbidden for the ghetto-dweller. The latter—mating with non-Kosher flesh—is the true consequence of the Faustian pact, and it determines what is the discriminated subject of Singer's novel: the character of freedom, the nature of slavery, and their tangential linkage depending on the inner life of Jacob. Such considerations give Singer a wide range of contemporary tensions to deal with, especially important since his novels are chiefly historical and might otherwise lend themselves to dated philosophical assumptions.

It is not unusual that Jacob's lust for a Gentile should be presented amidst the orgiastic race from which Wanda springs. Racially, she is identifiable with Hell's inmates, the dwarfs and amputees of mismated parents, Bosch-like creatures upon whom God's wrath has already fallen. Her father, Bzik, and those like him are clearly not a chosen race. To move among the Bziks of this world, to be entranced by the magic of a Wanda, is to enter into a pact with one's baser desires. All this is particularly ironic for Jacob, who historically gained Isaac's blessing at the expense of the primitive Essau.

Thus the first element of Jacob's inner slavery is his inability to maintain his Jewish identity and remain ascetic in the face of threats to his race and his past history. Wanda is, of course, a flower among these desert plants, but nevertheless she is tainted by *her* race, her family. She may convert, but it is incomplete. She may assume another identity, but it proves temporary. For in that most intimate moment, when she is to bring life into the world perhaps at the expense of her own, Jacob fears she will reveal herself. And she does. At the moment when survival itself— his, the child's, now hers—is at issue, she cries out. Her disguise (as well as punishment) of self-enforced muteness must desert her when it is most needed.

Jacob, of course, is drawn even more deeply into deception. For one living a lie, both slavery and lib-

erty assume the same significance. Once free in Jose-
fov, he is as much a slave as he was formerly while
working Bzik's property. With freedom goes deception; with deception goes a form of servitude. Now,
then, can Jacob avoid the thralldom which seems his
lot?

Freedom in Singer's work is rarely freedom *from*,
but freedom *to*. That is to say, he flirts with modern
themes, without committing himself to a modernistic
point of view. "Freedom from" is easily a cheap political slogan, a rallying cry, a simplistic phrase indicating
what one does *not* have to be or do. "Freedom to" is
the philosopher's cry—the phrase indicating what one
can be, *sui generis*. Singer dances around the latter
phrase, finding in it sanctions for temptation and excuses for loss of faith, but he also uncovers there what
is attractive about human tenacity. At their own expense, Jacob and others like him must be free to
choose, free to seek whatever Zion there may be, free
to twist and turn in the hope of discovering the path
of righteousness.

Lust, physical appetites, hope of guiltless joy—all
imprison. Enjoyment outside of traditional law, what
one is entitled to by birth, is short-lived, if at all
possible, and brings only sorrow. There is a real fear in
Singer of "freedom to," and yet there is the desire to
avoid the triviality of "freedom from." Always, there
is the sense of guilt in one's immediate background or
in the racial past. Guilt about flesh, guilt for one's
transgression, guilt toward one's father. Not sin,
which is a more conditioned response, but guilt—the
actual stuff built into the ethnic consciousness.

This emerging fear or anxiety extends into every
aspect of Singer's work, so that modern trends must
be resisted as one resists loss of faith and loss of
direction. Asa Heshel Bannet, in *The Family Moskat*,

represents the divided aims and sick hurry of the modernizing age, full of "light half-bclievers of our casual creeds." But Asa is no scholar gypsy; he seeks his soul in a succession of adoring women and aimless pursuits, and in so doing loses whatever identity he has. All that is left is to wait for the Messiah of Death in the shape of the German millennium.

In these respects, *The Slave* is a paradigm of Singer's fiction. Jacob acts out his secret desires when he succumbs to Wanda and then allies himself to her. She is the "forbidden fruit," the tainted meat which poisons even though she is packaged prettily. Her conversion is simply a façade for the guile that operates to destroy Jacob, her obedience and obeisance cloaks for the Devil's temptations. Wanda herself is innocent, of course, but Jacob in this male novel must make the final decisions.

As long as Jacob lives with secret desires, both before and after marriage, he is doomed. Even his affections are corroded. When he returns for Wanda, "She looked smaller and thinner than she had been, more like a girl than a woman." Physically, the reality is a hoax; his lust is a remembered pleasure. The present calls for rejection, and yet he is tied to his image of her. Singer destroys pleasure even as the mind conjures with it.

Joy, as we have seen, must be channeled. Once Wanda has been sacrificed to the delivery of a future Messiah, Jacob must return to the ways of his people in Palestine. The morality of the Patriarchs is clear: the woman serves as a secondary creature whose function is solely familial and whose self-assertion makes a man ridiculous or remiss. In a larger sense, all of Singer's fictions are family novels, in which the man is the Father of the Race, the woman a grieving, sacrificial soul, or a straying creature who must be rejected, the son devout or erring. If erring, the son may stray, as Asa Heshel does, or he may, like Jacob, pass through the three stages of Everlasting No, Center of Indifference, and Everlasting Yea—that is, be redeemed through faith in himself and in the future of his religion. If devout, the son may be torn by fleshly desires or may sweat through the Faustian quest for experience, which he tries to repress in the study house.

In the modern world, man is doomed apparently to thread a drunken path unless he is anchored to something more substantial than lust, whim, or appetite. This much is obvious: the substance of nearly every form of contemporary fiction from Dostoevsky and Conrad through Camus and Malraux. Ultimately, the character who tries to resolve these dilemmas must seek deeply within, without any assurance of success. Camus' Meursault floats slackly in a Christian world whose every semblance Jacob fears; and yet Jacob, once he breaks away from the traditional past, enters Meursault's anomic hell. The secular Yasha, the magician of Lublin, is another version of the same fate. Half Jew, half Gentile, Yasha moves uneasily among earthly pleasures. The others have their God and their saints—"he had only doubt." Ridiculing the soul, mocking the afterlife, believing in natural law, he fears everything but with picaresque escapades disguises his anxiety. He is lost, as lost as Jacob when he too begins to move uneasily between Jewish stricture and Gentile indulgence.

Man, says Singer, is made for one world only—that which he is born into, trained for, oriented toward by family, religion, and temperament. One stays in his father's court; the family orbit, despite friction, saves. Without is crisis, loss of face, even of soul, possible damnation amidst fires and pitchforks. The ghetto means safety based on restriction. Man's appetites need external restraints, or else he moves toward uncontrollable dangers. In the Author's Note to *In My Father's Court*, Singer writes of the Beth Din in which he grew up as a kind of refuge where justice and love were dispensed, a "blend of a court of law, synagogue, house of study, and if you will, psychoanalyst's office where people of troubled spirit could come to unburden themselves." Ruling the court as a benevolent despot is the father, whose right of rule reverts through the Talmudic interpreters to Moses himself.

To regain our Faustian analogy: the Beth Din is Faust's study, the safe place to which he is temperamentally suited. To seek outside is to tempt spiritual disaster. Beth Din, the ghetto, the study or study house, the ritual bath—these have been tested; they must be continued unless society disintegrate into anomic individuals.

Such views are of course relevant to *The Slave*. Like Yasha, Jacob is on the verge of becoming a "magician" or confidence man; this will, in fact, be his fate if he retains his mask. If Jacob is, as his name indicates, *the* Jew, then his sufferings and quest are those of all Jews, and his salvation lies in finding a place where a pariah can be a *Mensch*.

A modern parable is in the making: or at least until Jacob finds the path of righteousness and "suffers through" to salvation. There is the feel of truth in Jacob's and Sarah's (Wanda's) relationship to each other and to the society in which they move. Paradoxically, "Sacred though the truth was, the law did not permit one to sacrifice oneself for it." One's inner life becomes circumscribed by irony, paradox, fate; squeezed out or pushed into a tiny corner of existence is the truth about the individual and his connection to his immediate reality.

For Singer, this type of perversion cannot continue, though he is able to define it very tellingly. With a fertile conception of the fantastic, a verbal Chagall, a post-surrealist poet, cavorting verbally and imagistically with apocryphal visions, he nevertheless sees the fantastic only as antecedent to an opening out into truth. Put another way, the Dionysian appears to predominate, with its images of satyrs cavorting with men, of licentious women, of a world given to boldness, with Mephistopheles in the shape of one's appetites. From this, the Apollonian soul develops slowly, as torment, guilt, sin. Those saved find their home; those damned continue elsewhere.

It is here that Singer must confront the secular reader and such readers must confront Singer. It is here that one must reckon with the *shtetl* ideology that curls around his every word and scene and suggests a nineteenth-century attention to solutions. The reader must himself take care not to be automatically suspicious of a contemporary fiction that synthesizes man's fate in terms of personal faith, directed will, or final arbitration. Perhaps in our continued adherence to a purposeless universe in which our roles seem related more to chance than to design, we have become blinded to this element of directed experience. Singer evidently recognizes the broad sense of aimlessness in our lives. *The Slave* depends on it. In one particularly moving part, when Jacob is yearning for Wanda, when his dead wife and children are receding, when personal desire mingles with "mackerel-crowded" nature, Singer writes: "From somewhere far off came a muted yodel. A cowherd was singing in the foul dampness, and his distant voice pleased and demanded, lamented the injustice visited on all living things: Jews, gentiles, animals, even the flies and gnats crawling on the hips of the cattle."

For many engaged contemporary writers, this would be an existential moment. In this view, stung by loss of purpose, Jacob would have to come to terms with the void. His salvation, in fact, would depend not on his finding any "solution," however tenuous, but in revising his expectations appropriate to a skew world. Singer, on the contrary, makes Jacob move *against* not *with* the experience. He refuses to cut him off, even though all phenomena—Wanda, nature, the sound of the yodel—indicate that his fall means nothing, that his very existence is nullity.

Jacob declines to succumb, but even if we find his resurrection in Palestine too easy an escape, it is his holding on that we must confront. In Singer, destiny and freedom are interrelated, not distinct. We are faced, then, by a contradiction between what is true to life and what we assume to be the truth of art. In art, we are almost immediately suspicious of any resolution leading to human satisfaction or fulfillment, while we expect life to yield to individual will, to be structured on layers of order. Paradoxically, we ask our fictional protagonists not to surrender that quality of moral choice which differentiates man from animals, and yet we lock them into a system where they must suffer without complaint, or else complain without hope of escape.

Singer questions these assumptions. Arguing for traditional values, he poses disturbing questions *because* he runs counter to so much of current—and unavoidable—pessimism. He appears to feel for things with different nerve endings; that he writes in Yiddish is simply the verbal indication of the other world which engages him. Yet the more we learn about human nature, the more that sociologists, psychiatrists, even statisticians, tell us, the clearer it is that most people are closer to Singer's mode than to the one presented by our other major European writers. Put another way, Singer is their consciousness, only to surface sporadically.

We live by decisions that do seem, for most, to *resolve* problems, however imperfectly; we exist with expectations which do stand a chance of being fulfilled, or at least seem so when we cut our hopes; we have faiths (not faith) and we maintain them in the teeth of the most horrible onslaughts of human behavior—Poland's pogroms, Germany's "final solution," America's atomizing and napalming of innocents. Despite chaos without, we come through to grapple with our own needs: tax returns, house building, car buying, rising prices—as the response of the healthy man's ego to its own survival. The sensitive among us feel self-hatred for this ability to remain stable, and yet the fat, rich American is our self-image.

Singer touches us probingly in this area. He writes at the level of our ordinary lives. Jacob will make decisions, he will rearrange his life to seek solutions, he will find a haven from the coming disaster. In presenting Jacob's affirmative response, Singer confronts the assimiliated American-Jewish reader: Given Jacob's situation, would he flee to Palestine or await Armageddon in Poland? Even if we find Jacob's flight to Jerusalem a solution outside instead of confrontation within, it is the kind of flight—to the suburbs, to changes of name, to interfaith marriages—that characterizes many Americans, and not least those who are disturbed by Jacob's positive interpretation of his own needs.

# The Piety of Things in *The Manor*

MARY ELLMANN

The modern history of the Jews may explain the nostalgia, but not the certitude, of I. B. Singer's writing. In *The Family Moskat,* he mourns the death of the Polish Jews, but in *The Manor* he mourns their lives before their deaths. One retains from *The Family Moskat* an excruciating pleasure in the idiom, the idiosyncrasies, the vital imperfections of its finally ruined people. And, of course, there is still a fondness for personality in *The Manor.* But it is now a curtailed and subordinate source of interest. Characters come forward and recede in short, simple, even perfunctory turns. Each is quickly comprehensible, and thereafter consistent. Thoughts and feelings are obvious rather than labyrinthine. The psychological complexity to which we are habituated is put aside like an irrelevance. The familiarity, even the reiteration, of human experience is apparent, rather than its ingenuity. Always the two horses of a waiting team put their heads together as though to exchange secrets. Always young men copy their first love letters out of manuals of letter-writing. Someone always worries, What *is* gravity? And each successive matrix of details is not only familiar, but exceptionally distant. This is a distance of judgment, of an abiding moral assessment.

Ostensibly, *The Manor* concerns itself with the proliferative historical changes affecting the lives of Polish Jews in the last quarter of the nineteenth century. Singer himself lists these changes in a preface: "socialism and nationalism, Zionism and assimilationism, nihilism and anarchism, suffragetism, atheism, the weakening of the family bond, free love, and even the beginnings of Fascism." The jumble is significant: in the novel, these concepts are granted none of their conventional importance. They seem interchangeable, indistinguishable here—conglomerate distractions from piety. In this sense, *The Manor* is a profoundly irrational book, and yet its effect is one of extreme order and arrangement. The two qualities coexist in this way: separations, distinctions, contrasts pervade the work, but these are religious, not intellectual.

The central character is Jewry rather than Calman Jacoby. From Calman's God, divine nerves run out through all the universe. A system of subtle and evanescent, and yet solemn, intercommunications is thus established between God and moon, man and cricket, God and man. The imbalance is such, however, that neither God nor the rain can make a mistake. Only the Jew is capable of error, of impiety, as only he is capable of piety. His religion, through which his God has been codified, shares (even as it envelops) the utter rightness of snow or spring. Nonetheless, to the simple person who wants to be pious, God and nature may sometimes seem to be at odds. To the clever, secular person, the two are a senseless distinction— everything to him, including man, is nature. And, in its own way, *The Manor* agrees—indeed, everything lapses into nature upon the dismissal of religion. In that condition, childbirth and nationalism—or, for that matter, fascism—are identical, and both in turn identical with meat or maggots. But for those who attain piety, everywhere is Israel and all created matter is Jewish:

The branches of the trees resembled crystal menorahs. Candles were ignited in them by the setting sun and then extinguished.

So nature, including human nature, is more emblematic in *The Manor* than loosely associative. Singer's snowstorms always form minute domes on gateposts, and sunsets redden all his early evenings. But while in *The Magician of Lublin*, the sunset is associated with blood, and in *The Family Moskat* with fire, in *The Manor* it is precisely a "celestial holocaust," a word which insists upon, rather than suggesting, the genocide of the Jews. So too, in *The Family Moskat*, the attraction of moths to a street lamp suggested, simply enough, the reckless attraction of Asa Heshel and Hadassah to each other. "Midges, butterflies and moths" perform a similar duty in *The Manor* —when Calman Jacoby is attracted to the gentile servant, Antosia, and when his second wife, Clara, is attracted to the university student, Alexander Zipkin. But here, a parallel is established between the two moments, and both in turn are related to other juxtapositions of insect and human being. The moths are faultless in their suicide—all subhuman life is faultless and, to those of refined perception, expressive of God. The young rabbi, Jochanan, tries to feed the butterfly which lights on his "holy book" and trembles with joy when two flies mate on his table: "All living things united, the small as well as the large. Everything was either male or female." In *The Family Moskat*, another rabbi has a similar experience: "The rabbi looked at the goat, and the goat stared back at him. He suddenly felt a rush of affection for the creature, the 'valiant among the grass-eaters,' which the Talmud compared to Israel, the 'valiant among the nations.' He felt like caressing the poor beast or giving it some tasty tidbit." Like Jochanan, this rabbi too wants to feed the creature he loves. In *The Manor*, however, the flies are not associated with anything, even a holy place. They stand for the holy sexuality of all living forms.

Lesser persons than Jochanan move myopically through the same world. Their joy in it is roused infrequently, and only by spectacular manifestations —the explosion of spring, the blatant fecundity of summer. It is the reader, more often than the character, who is allowed to see with Jochanan-like eyes. Arriving at his son-in-law's mill, Calman Jacoby is conscious only of having broken with his wife Clara— which is, for him, to have begun again to be pious. As he walks through the mill yard, a ladybug settles on his lapel. Though Calman pays no attention, the insect is part of his re-entry into proportion. The lust of flies is as innocent as it is indiscriminate. Subhuman life can neither offend nor worship God through fornication. But the Jew in *The Manor* must choose, and it is at the moment Calman resumes the discrimination which the insect need not have, that he and the ladybug are both exquisite (and therefore coincident) forms of life.

Ordinarily, nature not only obscures its meanings, but tests the capacity of men in turn to retain separate meanings. It is understood that external circumstances change without deliberation (winter does not *decide* to foreclose summer), and that human moods tend to answer, to shift with the seasons or the hours of the day. This evocative power of nature is, as ever in Singer, beautiful in *The Manor*, but even more treacherous. The scene still lures the feeling, but the novel attaches itself to the beauty, not of the passive response, but of the moral force which chooses whether to yield or deny.

Physical happiness is not, for this reason, deplored.

On the contrary, as in the gentile Dante, sheer sullen-
ness is a fault. Observing the growth of plants and the
movement of domestic animals, Calman Jacoby takes
heart. Even when his situation logically indicates anxiety, he responds to the tangible evidences of hope.
There is always this resurgent good nature in Singer—
his work exemplifies what he has called "that Polish-
Jewish look of hopefulness that no misfortune could
efface." He finds it in simple people, and misses it in
the boredom and depression of the educated. It seems
his child side, an ineradicable pleasure in freshness, in
all beginnings. Even here, in this severe book, young
love is allowed some pathetic turmoil, and young children are still eager and agile, shinnying up poles and
trees to see everything from fires to funerals. But their
vivid responses are diminished in adulthood, which
defines itself as a set of distinctions between impulse
and virtue. In the forest at night, Calman's restraint
of his desire for the servant Antosia is what we would
call now "unnatural," puritanical. It is the opposite of
his wife Clara's acquiescence in the company of
Zipkin:

> The place was dusty. Two brass candlesticks stood on
> the sheet-draped piano as if at the head of a corpse. As
> she moved around the unfamiliar room, inspecting the
> pictures and knickknacks, Clara felt both fear and de-
> sire. Zipkin had wandered off somewhere. The air was
> heavy with the odor of camphor. The dry furniture
> squeaked, and she felt warm and sticky. A moth began
> to flutter about the candle Zipkin had lit.

Both Calman and Clara absorb close and compelling
emanations of place. And Clara's close ("warm and
sticky") desire exudes in response. But this is a corre-
spondence which the novel, even in the notice of the
corpse-piano, forewarns of deadliness. Strictness, per-
versely, is the means of continued avidity for life. The

"twittering birds" rouse Calman to his work in the morning from a fast, dreamless sleep; Clara, hearing the same sound ("birds chirping") in the morning after Zipkin, turns her face to the wall. What she thought, apart from what she felt, in the empty drawingroom, was not "All for love," but, "I mustn't die here." She remarks to Zipkin, "Sometimes I think the whole world is a cemetery," and the same night she dreams of being "mortally ill." Separated later from Calman and pregnant by Zipkin, she envies mannequins in a store window: "What's wrong with being a doll like that? . . . They don't even know they exist."

While one cannot exaggerate the primness with which Clara's transgressions are judged in the novel, it is not an ascetic revulsion. All processes of the body, aberrant as well as normal, are acknowledged. The first wife Zelda's legs swell, an infant is born without a stomach, and lazy Celina Frankel lives to fill her chamber pot with excrement and menstrual blood. Menstruation, as an "unclean" aspect of nature, is a conspicuous marital problem. Zelda Jacoby takes the ritual baths of purification. Clara, the secular sophisticate, laughs at them. Sexual intercourse itself is a religious act, required of saints as of houseflies. Even Clara is inclined to grant marriage its sanctity, or at least its security: "From flirting to behold-you-are-consecrated is quite a jump." Then how, in describing marriage, is the novelist himself to be at once natural and pious? By delicate regard: pious wives are awarded pious words. No woman is undressed in *The Family Moskat* except Hadassah, who commits adultery during the Ten Penitential Days: "Her nipples were a fiery-red color." And it is only Clara in *The Manor* whose breasts are visible through her nightdress as she paces a bedroom, lying to Calman.

Natural appetites are sanctified as duties. The Jews must couple and they must eat meat, by law. Therefore they must kill animals. If there were no other, this grim prerogative alone would set them apart from the prey, even as it obliges them to recognize and to encounter it. In pure recognition, there is potential love of the animal. But in every encounter, there must be ritual and law to suppress an equally potential cruelty. Therefore hunting in *The Manor* is gentile, savage—there cannot be a proper killing for sport. Even the dog, since it is associated with attack, seems gentile, "anti-Semitic" in its ferocity alone. ("Dogs? They are not just dogs. They're the hounds of Egypt.") When Calman Jacoby has to go into the forest ("fit for wolves, not men"), he provides himself with two dogs and a gun—and so compromises with savagery, with gentile "might." Just by having a gun in his hut at night, he defiles the proper circumstances of prayer. Perhaps the only legitimate function of the Singer dog is barking at baleful times. It shares this duty of omen with the cawing crow—and both, in this one way, participate in virtue, vocalizing misdemeanors to all who will listen.

But it is particularly Count Wladislaw Jampolski—the lord of the manor, the gentile, the patriot, the atheist, the sensualist, the Darwinist—who is also the hunter. (His hunting dogs, Wilk and Piorun, leap at Miriam Lieba, Calman's third daughter, when she enters the manor.) It is also Jampolski, returned from political exile, who describes the Siberians who hunt bears with clubs. If that is courage, *The Manor* implies, let Jews be timid. Jampolski tolerates all natural encounters, all degrees of violent contact—between men and animals, men and women, even men and bedbugs. He doesn't enjoy being *bitten* by bedbugs, but he enjoys discussion of the biting—for the torment it inflicts upon his daughter, the unhappy Felicia, and for itself. Jampolski's bedbugs become, in this way, the tiny demons who oppose the tiny angels, Calman's ladybug and Jochanan's butterfly—as his obscene pleasure in infestation has also to be set against Abram Shapiro's reverence in *The Family Moskat*: "God feeds all things, from the giant elephant to the eggs of the louse."

Jampolski's tolerance is perverse, the corruption of what Singer has called "natural loathing." For the louse, there can be properly only the divine tenderness of which Abram Shapiro is in awe, or human hostility. Those creatures which are allied with danger, filth, and disease—wolves, dogs, snakes, worms, fleas, lice, lizards, rats, and mice—endure a flagrant ostracism in *The Manor*. Rabbi Menachem Mendel is shocked by his son Ezriel's childhood interest, which seems to us unexceptional, in "frogs and other unclean reptiles." When Calman Jacoby wakes in Jochanan's house "burning with lust" for Clara, he hears a mouse "gnawing at the floorboards like a creature with a saw in its jaws." He pounds a boot against the bed and says, "Be still, devil"—as Jochanan, burning with love, sprinkled sugar in a drop of tea and said to the butterfly, "Drink."

Yet both men *speak*, to the despicable as to the beautiful creature. In limited lives, there remains a closeness even to those living things which are outcast, and the minds of Singer's characters swarm like zoos with animal images. Mrs. Frankel complains at night, "If everyone isn't in the house, I toss and turn like a worm." The girl Kasia's mother, Stachowa, screams at Kasia's father: "Pig! Dog! Hyena!" A mental patient imagines at every meal that her plate is heaped with lice. The peasant women remark, "A man is like a dog. . . . Feed him, give him a place to sleep, and he won't leave his kennel." Dying, even the saintly rabbi of Marshinov sees demons "disguised as frogs, lizards, skunks, vipers, with horns and snouts, with claws and tails, with elephant trunks and boar tusks." In this way, the worst are like the best: Lucian Jampolski too, on the verge of being caught by the police, dreams that an ape has him by the throat. The ape is in favor, especially among the liberals, thanks to Darwin. The Count, Lucian's father, proceeds to prove the theory by retrogressive practice, by evolving backwards—encaging himself, reversing day and night until he is nocturnal, and mating with the servant Antosia, who ate grains of wheat from Calman's straw mattress and slept in his stable. Jampolski's favorite word is *psiakrew*—dog's blood.

Jampolski is happily rid of all distinctions except those pertaining to blue blood—*noble* descendants of the ape do not receive *shoemaker* descendants of the ape. But the poorest Jew in the novel remains a Jew by means of separations and distinctions, by avoiding fusions. Jochanan's sense of creative unity, distributed among all Jews, would degenerate into sentimentality or brutality—the vulgar twins. Therefore he does not dwell on unity, and even he is obliged to take part in the ritual slaughter of roosters and hens—as, in fact, rabbis then answered dietary and sexual questions too, assessing between commentaries the menstrual stains on women's lice-infested underwear. But Jochanan can hardly discipline his dread. Though he believes, and so should be glad, that migrant human souls may be set free from the dead fowl (as walking souls were believed to leave the imprint of fowl on the earth), he hates to grab the rooster by its legs and to feel its terror. As he has been enabled to "rejoice with trembling," the rooster fears with trembling. But then, as the two share the physical sensation, so they might, at any moment, exchange these separate ecstasies of joy and terror. "Slaughterer, knife, rooster were identical," all aspects of the creation which the ritual destruction honors: "There was no death."

In contrast to Jochanan, Ezriel Babad, as a child, objects to Elisha's having set the bears on the children, and to the agony of the carp as it is scaled alive for the Sabbath meal. His rabbi-father sees in this humane objection, the questioning of faith. Ezriel would change the Sabbath in order to change the carp's fate —as Abraham, if he had been entirely the humane father, would have disobeyed God in order to save Isaac. But Ezriel's alliance with nature, however pure in its original sympathy, does not enable him in *The Manor* to replace agony and death by ease and life. On the contrary, in the course of the novel, he sees death thrive in his secular society, like a disease against which unseen antibodies have lost their efficacy. Death merely sheds the element of sanctification which clung to the carp's scaling. The child Sasha, within the next Jewish generation, tortures and drowns his pets for play. (His last gesture in the novel is to snatch at the last butterfly in the novel.) And the adult Ezriel sums up the practice of medicine and of revolutionary politics, through which he and his sister have sought the alleviation of pain: "Now he spent his time cutting the dead apart, and Mirale plotted to kill the living." What is gained, *The Manor* asks, by preventing diphtheria and tuberculosis? Beneath this happy "Heraclitean change," this diversion of germs, two essences remain the same: religious piety and its opposite, natural cruelty. In the absence of piety, assumed among the gentiles and deplored among the Jews, the novel foresees all those future clear-lunged Jews who were to breathe gas and burn in fire.

Jews like Ezriel—clean-shaven, serious, anxious, studious world-improvers—are pitied because they are always disappointed. They take less joy from Kant and Rousseau than the unworldly Jew from his phylacteries. Asa Heshel Bannet, student of Nietzche in *The Family Moskat*: "I've made up my mind that the human race is no more important than flies and bedbugs." And Ezriel Babad, released from irrational faith, can discern no direction of the world except irrational chance.

But what Ezriel considers accidental is mysteriously directed in *The Manor*, just as the crows seem to caw by secret appointment. What looks like chance may be the Hassidic miracle—not the outlandish ghost or dybbuk, but miracle traveling incognito, through seemingly natural forms and events. After his third daughter, Miriam Lieba, has refused to have Jochanan as a husband, Calman Jacoby substitutes his fourth daughter, the eleven-year-old Tsipele, as the future bride. In doing so, he is conscious of embarrassment before Jochanan's relatives, of compromise, even of injustice, since Tsipele (the "little chick," the "calf") is patently too young for the sexual context into which Calman propels her, and too young to demand the independent choice which Miriam Lieba had been allowed. Nonetheless, Calman has behaved properly by religious, if not by modern, standards. And the marriage of Jochanan and Tsipele, against what seems even the novel's expectation, is its most nearly perfect. Was it then only physical chance that Miriam Lieba did not take to Jochanan? Or that Calman had at hand a fourth daughter? (A genetic *mis*chance, in most parents' eyes.) Calman does not think of the marriage as extraordinary—to do so would be to consider himself the agent, or at least the recipient, of miracle. And yet, the implication is that miracle, like a blush, may be the sudden suffusion of chance by piety.

Piety is the sole insurance not only of philosophical order but also of practical good. Ezriel's humanism results in his misdirection of others as well as of himself. He objects that the Torah overlooks "human emotion, man's nervous system," and becomes a psychiatrist instead of a rabbi. Two persons then, both afflicted by emotional (or nervous? or chemical?) problems, present themselves: one to Ezriel, the other to Jochanan. Ezriel's patient is an impotent bridegroom. Ezriel recommends hydrotherapy (the emancipated ritual bath?) and pockets his forty-kopeck fee. Jochanan's visitor is puzzled by conflicting diagnoses of his daughter's stomach pains. Should she have surgery or not? But Jochanan knows nothing about medicine. He gives the man his gold watch to pay a third specialist who may arbitrate the opinions of the first two. And he promises that the girl will recover because—"reason" enough—her father asks to be promised.

Ezriel, at this moment of Polish-Jewish change, becomes an intellectual. But the life of the brain is strictly equivalent in *The Manor* to the life of any other part of the body—to the life, say, of the vagina to which Clara Jacoby turns. Ezriel exchanges piety for thought, Clara for sensation—for what she calls (with exemplary modernism) "experience"—a lover because she has had only husbands before. But that her and Ezriel's routes must converge is indicated by Ezriel's advancing toward adultery also. On the balcony where he kisses the widow Olga Bielikov, the two plan to look at the stars through a telescope. It is a relic of Olga's dead husband who had also been (almost) a scientist, a home astronomist. The affair with Olga promises to be subtle, cultivated. She has a small daughter who plays the piano and a highstrung son, whose screaming in the night Ezriel diagnoses (with exemplary professionalism) as "Pavor nocturnus." (The next time the child screams, his mother will soothe him with a term.) And after all, Shaindel, Ezriel's wife, is pregnant for the fifth time, ignorant, fat, frigid. But going home, as the horse stops at his gate, Ezriel thinks:

> How wonderful animals are compared to humans! They have everything—humility, serenity, faith, inner detachment.

And no notion of the stars. Naturally, as Ezriel goes in the gate, a dog barks. And as he climbs the dark stairs, he thinks he sees a demon with the legs of a goose.

From the portentous West, *The Manor*'s Jews contrast new uses of life. Ezriel responds to abstract, Calman Jacoby to concrete, innovation. To produce railroad ties, he depletes a forest. His lime kiln scarifies the land and dirties the air. The "chaos and babble" he dislikes in Warsaw, he introduces in the village of Jampol. The exploitation of nature proves to be an exploitation of the self—unwittingly, Calman alters all that he had liked as it was.

This delusion of "development," like the delusion of "experience," is traced with the transparency, but also the confidence, of a medieval exemplum. In poverty, Calman was a peddler. He dressed in the long Jewish caftan. His house in the ghetto was small and bare—Singer furnishes its inventory in two sentences. Calman's stomach digested simple food: cottage cheese, dark bread and water for breakfast, buckwheat grits for supper, and for his first trip to Warsaw, a chicken "wrapped in cabbage leaves." Even his sexual life was poor—between her illnesses and her menstrual punctilio, Zelda, the first wife, was a model of insufficiency.

All this is changed by wealth. *The Manor* is charged with an undeviating dislike of sophistication—its most abusive, and much repeated, adjective is *elegant*. To supervise his enterprises, Calman begins to ride horseback—a manorial, elegant, gentile exercise in itself, fit for the Jampolskis and for Clara and Zipkin, who mount each other so readily in turn. But for Calman to ride, it is necessary to discard the caftan for a jacket. A testamentary shortening: spirit is abstracted from matter, piety from the length of the coat and the beard. For women, from the degree of self-neglect. Like the dishevelled Natasha at the end of *War and Peace*, the excellent woman remains for Singer the distracted wife, her matron's wig perched askew on her cropped head. But in *The Manor*, Jews cease to state their religion in their dress and come to resemble gentiles—to whom they remain Jews. In this sense, the gentiles expose the fallacy, for Singer, of assimilation. They will not allow the Jew to be a gentile, Singer will not allow him to be merely human. There is not a chance in *The Manor* between being a Jew and being Everyman, only between imitating God or imitating animals. Calman's first luxury is a "fox-lined overcoat with little tails dangling from the inner seams."

Calman begins to be often away from home—in the forest, or in the jungle of Warsaw. The affection for this city which *The Family Moskat* expresses in its meticulous tracing of houses, streets and gardens, is erased in *The Manor*. Here, deprived of particulars, Warsaw summarized human indifference, frivolity, despair. The droshky horses bear down on the crowds, the pitch of trade is crazy, the Vistula is a synonym for suicide. In the clutter of streets, the young provincial Ezriel loses his way and is too late for the ritual bathing. It is in Warsaw that Calman Jacoby eats in restaurants, does business with the converted Jew, Wallenberg, and (as it seems, consequently) marries his second wife, Clara. With Clara, Calman finds himself moving into the manor itself, the summit of the local gentile culture. He is afraid of slipping on the polished parquet floors. The furnishings of his original home were required, by physical necessity or religious ritual. Now Calman is surrounded by objets d'art. References to these things in *The Manor* are exceedingly morose—one would think some soul in Gehenna had been set the penance of museum guide.

All artistic representations are associated with irreligion. The gilded lions on the ark of the Torah are the one exception, and even these ("tails up and tongues protruding") distract the young Ezriel from his yeshivah studies. Clara, hunting for Zipkin in Warsaw, stares listlessly at "pagan" statuary in a bookshop window. (In *The Family Moskat*, Nyunie's ill-tempered second wife polishes the belly of a Buddha in *her* bookshop.) And at the convert Wallenberg's house, Ezriel, who hungered for pictures as a child, studies an oil painting—without profit. The "experience" is no longer denied and no longer pleasing. The theme of hunting recurs in the painting: a wounded deer leaves a trail of blood on snow. As a matter of fact, the deer's whole life lies within the novel. When Mayer Joel, Calman's first son-in-law, walked through the fields of winter wheat during his first visit to Jampol, he caught sight of a deer—a real deer, of course, at the edge of a real forest. Later, in the same fields, the daughter Miriam Lieba, mooning for her gentile lover, hears a shot. A hunter? she thinks. Or war? A hunter, according to Wallenberg's painting, but one need not distinguish exactly between commingling modes of violence.

So much for Singer's own preoccupation, literature, as well. With Clara in tow, Zipkin talks about "love, literature, money, and the situation in Russia." Miriam Lieba reads French love stories and complains that the lives of Jews are "narrow and stagnant." From her behavior, Ezriel surmises that she is a victim of romance, of some perhaps improper passion—could she be in love with *him*, her brother-in-law? "From reading Slowacki and other poets, Ezriel knew that love obeys no laws." And the girl whom Zipkin marries, the idle and possessive Sabina, sits in an all-blue bedroom reading, or pretending to read, a book of poems. She sends Zipkin away and then, like a librarian, recalls him—along with an overdue copy of Musset.

Even colors are sectarian: blue is gentile, black is Jewish. In *The Manor*, the Jewishness which the Jew is tempted to put off is an essential darkness or burden of the spirit. So Ezriel, separating himself from the Jews, thinks, "I must help these people emerge from darkness," and in the disorder of Calman's world, dimness is the lost design. When he was poor, he used a "solitary tallow candle" and Zelda lighted the Sabbath candles. When Calman is rich, he is "enlightened." Secular candlesticks sprout up everywhere, like fungi, around him; and groping about in the dark when he determines to leave Clara, he is obliged, for his mistakes, to bump into a candelabrum. Meanwhile, Miriam Lieba has eaten a last Purim feast with her family by the harsh light of a new naphtha lamp. She eats very little, her mind is bloated with love. Ezriel recites the prayer ("Young lions do lack and suffer hunger"), and after the meal, the young lions, Lucian and Miriam Lieba, meet outside in the clear night: "the stars burned like lanterns in mid-air." By early morning, Calman and Shaindel realize from her empty room that Miriam Lieba has run away: "Night still clung to the room, but the sunrise had already begun to touch it." Moving about, the two are touched by light—"Calman's beard seemed bloodied; a red stain appeared on Shaindel's handkerchief." Illumination—enlightenment—will be death.

It is alien to us now, the preference of the novel for darkness and weight. But for the Jews in *The Manor*, the identification of light and lightness with the gentile and the godless, is inexorable. Calman himself has a thick-set body, dark beard and, dark eyes. Black tufts of hair, like secondary sidelocks, grow out of his ears. Zelda, the first wife, can hardly walk on her heavy, swollen legs. The daughter Shaindel is fatter after each of her deliveries. Holy obesity! Even cart horses in Singer come under this dispensation of weight, taking all the fondness denied the mounts. But Miriam Lieba, like Ezriel, is thin, blue-eyed and blonde— she looks like a gentile before she becomes one.

Her husband's name, Lucian, means "light," and Lucian's slender grace is the opposite of Calman's solidity. His clothing too is the farthest reach from the Jews' antiquated, awkward, "Asiatic" caftans. Lucian is a dandy, given to riding breeches, soft German boots, white shirts. From his various sties, he contrives, when he likes, to step out immaculately. When he is not afraid of syphilis, his body is like the manor house under Clara's care—too clean. (Shaindel's apartment is always untidy.) Lucian shines. After meeting him, Miriam Lieba imagines his reappearance: "He was bathed in an ethereal light, like the visions of saints described in books by Christian mystics." He could not, in *The Manor*, have chosen a more ominous guise. He himself, shutting his eyes, sees sparks of bright colors, shifting designs.

Lucian is always in movement. With him, Miriam Lieba (now Marisia) is the only member of her family who visits Dresden, Leipzig, Frankfurt, Paris. And it is through him, of course, that she has set sexuality (or its procurer, romance) before religious law. But if it is natural for love to be lawless, as the poet Slowacki said, why must Miriam Lieba live less naturally than an animal? She is constantly cold and hungry, she cannot even keep her young (her "future Jew-baiters," as her father thinks) with her. And what is travel? In Paris, Miriam Lieba encounters that same old international set of *The Manor*, "mice, bedbugs, fleas, flies, and beatles." And like Masha in *The Family Moskat*, she rocks with the gentile's alternations of idolatry and abuse—"that Jew bitch," Lucian calls her, the bitch who nonetheless enslaves the gentile dog. As always in Singer, sensuality plummets into enormity. Assimilated love, it seems, is doomed to fantasies of tyrants and slaves, pashas and harems. Lucian runs through all commonplace sensations and must devise quasi-criminal variants: it becomes essential to imagine killing whichever woman he is with.

His relationship with the child Kasia is the perversion of Calman's relationship with his daughter Tsipele. Kasia, also eleven, thinks of Lucian as a second father because he is living with her mother; and he speaks to her with authority, committing her to himself for their sexual future. Calman spoke of Tsipele gravely, committing her to Jochanan. His unexpressed desire was paternal—to take her on his knee, to prolong the childhood he was cancelling. Lucian's purpose, statutory rape, is accomplished when Kasia is fourteen. She is arrested in the hotel from which he has escaped. Lucian is forever escaping, returning, hiding, running from street to street, bed to bed, country to country. Even his nationalism, his part in the 1863 rebellion against Russia, is only an aspect of his congenital irritation, his unfocused need "to do something terrible, beat someone or find himself in some grand predicament."

So his committing murder seems at once accidental

and foreknown. On the night of his crime, he feels rather hungry, light-headed. His violence is avoidable, almost whimsical—these days, the murder would qualify as an *acte gratuit*. (Calman, with too much motive, decides not to murder Clara and Zipkin.) Lucian's victim ("the scurvy dog") delayed his leaving a courtyard—impeded his flight, his mobility. The simple removal of an impediment requires no discussion: Lucian, light years away from Raskolnikov, kills in a page or two, then leaves the novel. Someone mentions later that he is in prison, but soon to be released. Inevitably. Lucian *is* release, pure permission, the antithesis of "Don't do this, don't do that," which, as he remarks, is a "legacy from the Jews."

At one point, Lucian compares the world to a stew, a bubbling mess of things which, at any moment, God may shove all together through a sieve, and be done with it. But piety is a painstaking separation of one thing from another—dairy products from meat, menstruants from husbands, Sabbaths from workdays. It establishes, confined and forbids unions. Man is forbidden to be an animal, the Jew to be a gentile, the Hassid to be a positivist. Impiety is any substitution for piety—patriotism, psychiatry, apostasy, geography. "Asia here, Asia there. Meanwhile you forget to be Jews." The generic mark of the impious is a predilection for monism, for the assimilation of many forms into one. Zipkin: "Naked, we all stem from apes." The political scientist, Aaron Lipman: "Man is just another animal." The doctor, Zawacki: "We're all made of the same stuff." Lucian, to Kasia: "You call this liquor" It's water." Lucian, to Miriam Lieba: "What is snow? Water."

But snow to Miriam Lieba is the cause of the extreme cold, like a demonic draft, which reaches her in every meeting with Lucian before her marriage. Even in his brief absence, his glamor is associated with the fearful glamor of the faraway North Pole, which Ezriel describes. And yet, within Miriam Lieba's own home, the frost on the windowpane forms patterns of cedars and palms, images of warmth. And outdoors too, as long as she is near home, a snowstorm chides her, clouding her thoughts of Lucian with an incomprehensible melancholy. In the persistence of her attraction, she throws a snowball in the direction of the manor—as Ezriel, raging at the "darkness" of the Jews, flings a "hard ball" of snow against the twilight.

The end of Polish Jews like Miriam Lieba and Ezriel is foreshadowed by crossings and confusions within nature itself. The primary distinction removed, between Jews and other man, all distinctions blur. After adultery, Clara dreams of "half an orange, not yellowish gold as oranges usually are, but red." It suggests blood to her, a thing half fruit and half animal, and strangely sexual as well—the fruitful Jewess impregnated by sanguinary twentieth-century Europe. As Singer has written elsewhere: "The Cabbalists know that the passion for blood and the passion for flesh have the same origin, and this is the reason 'Thou shalt not kill' is followed by 'Thou shalt not commit adultery' " ("Blood" in *Short Friday*). Portents of blood and fire are ubiquitous in *The Manor*, involving the Jews and leading them, like flares in the dark, toward their own consumption. The delinquent Sasha sets fires. Punished by Calman for burning a haystack, he retaliates: "You dirty Jew!" The peasants talk of a "flaming witch" in the sky followed by "three fiery rams," and blame the drought on the Jews. When the Jews cease to believe that a salamander can live in fire, they themselves seem more certain to die in it.

But what if these Polish Jews had not been diverted

from Jewishness? What if they had all remained like the original, or even the reclaimed, Calman—simple and restricted, every action of their lives, eating, washing, cooking, mating, directed by religious rules? No one can believe that the Jews would not still have been murdered by the Nazis. The piety of the victim is rarely a deterrent to the victimizer. And Singer, of all writers, assumes that cruelty is always ready, provided at all times with alphabetical lists of the vulnerable. But the issue of *The Manor* is not that polemical favorite, What should the Jews have done differently in order to save their skins? Here, instead, there are implied differences in dying. The gentile murder of Jews who have lived in gentile manors, is considered an amorphous agony, an indeterminate part of the general slashing of men at men. The gentile murder of complete Jews is distinct, a crime of clarity. Ultimately, the Nazi criminal, like Lucian, is insubstantial, a disembodied blow. The substance, in *The Manor*, is piety—which renders the burned Jew, like the scaled carp, as sanctified as he is mutilated.

# Singer's Children's Stories and
## *In My Father's Court*
## Universalism and the Rankian Hero

H. R. WOLF

The predominant sense of space in I. B. Singer's autobiography, *In My Father's Court,* is one of enclosure and moral encapsulation. The world at large, the gentile world, defines itself as the landscape of transgression to the young Singer.

> The mummers, too, were disposed of quickly, for the wearing of masks and the singing of songs smacked of the theater, and the theater was *tref*—unclean. In our home, the "world" itself was *tref*.

And within the "unclean" circumference of the gentile world, the sacred space of the Rabbi's home itself can only, with great effort, be protected from the intrusions of the "worldly" Jewish community.

> For the sake of the business quarrels of these rich men he had had to give up time he would otherwise have devoted to the Torah, and he yearned for his books and commentaries. Once again the world with its calculations and falsehoods, had intruded into our life.

In the main, the movement of *In My Father's Court* charts the centrifugal journey out of enclosure, the journey towards nonparochial experience; three significant movements *out* in the autobiography characterize the expansion of self: the discovery of nature, the exposure to the bohemian, sensual atmosphere of his brother's studio, and the introduction to world literature.

Because of the spatial limitations of his father's house, the child's discovery of nature has about it a pristine and primal quality and, ironically, can be described only in terms commensurate to Genesis, to the vision of the Hebraic world. Despite this irony, one feels in reading the autobiography that the child will never be able to go home again in quite the same way after his visit "To The Wild Cows."

> I had not yet seen any wild cows, but what I had seen already was wonderful and strange. The sky here was not a narrow strip as on Krochmalna Street, but broad, spread out like the ocean, and it descended to the earth like a supernatural curtain. Birds flew overhead in swarms, with a twittering, a cawing, a whistling—large birds and small birds. Two storks were circling above one of the hills of the Citadel. Butterflies of all colors fluttered above the grass: white, yellow, brown, with all kinds of dots and patterns. The air smelled of earth, of grass, of the smoke of locomotives, and of something more that intoxicated me and made my head reel. There was a strange stillness here, and yet everything murmured, rustled, chirped. Blossoms fell from somewhere and settled on the lapels of my jacket. I looked up at the sky, saw the sun, the clouds, and suddenly I understood more clearly the meaning of the words of Genesis. (This, then, was the world God had created: the earth, the heavens, the waters above that are separated by the firmament from the waters below.)

The exposure to his brother's studio—to sensuous art and sensuous women—reveals the way in which the father's house had confined the senses, diminished the body, and supported guilt feelings.

> I visited my brother several times, but each visit startled me all over again. I was fascinated by the thought

of being in a room with a glass roof. Through the sky-
light I could glimpse blue sky, sun, and birds. Passover
had come and gone. The paintings and statues were
spangled with light. Every time I came, Ostrzego would
have to lift the moist sacks again so that I could see
the statues, which became more and more real for me,
as if the hunchback had breathed a soul into them.

I was astonished at the sight of naked breasts on the
figures of young and pretty girls, for I had assumed that
breasts were solely the property of slovenly women who
nursed babies in public. I had been brought up to believe that only a lecher observes such things, but I came
to realize that artists looked at them differently.

The third movement *out*, the introduction to world
literature, to imaginative experience beyond the limits
of the legalistic Talmud and Torah, becomes the basis
for a movement *in* towards the self. The lonely child
who has been envied by his peers for his "dreams"
discovers in nonparochial literature the joy and mystery that he associates with the Cabbala. At this point,
his father's mystical Judaism, as opposed to his mother's empirical temper, and Singer's creative *élan* meet.
But they meet only at a point. Ultimately, Singer's
exploration of the mysterious and irrational undercur-
rents of the mind are not coincident with his father's
world-view.

I grew accustomed to being alone and the days no
longer seemed interminable. I studied, wrote, read
stories. My brother had brought home a two-volume
book called *Crime and Punishment*. Although I didn't
really comprehend it, it fascinated me. Secluded in the
bedroom, I read for hours. A student who had killed a
crone suffered, starved, and reasoned profoundly. Coming before the prosecutor, he was questioned. . . . It
was something like a storybook, but different. . . .
Who were the authors of books like this, and who

could understand them? Now and then a passage became illuminated for me, I understood an episode, and
grew enthralled by the beauty of a new insight.

Although the movement *in* towards non-Judaic literature spirals towards seclusion, self-absorption, and fantasy; although this turning *in* constitutes a repudiation
of experience, in another sense a further expansion of
self, a further universalizing of consciousness, takes
place. Where responsibility began in dreams for
Yeats, we could say that for Singer pan-culturalism
begins in the mythic substratum of imaginative literature. Methodologically, there could be no sounder
testing ground for this premise than an examination
of Singer's children stories—that aspect of the adult
canon most closely approximating the enthralling effect of *Crime and Punishment* upon the young, proto-
writer.

An undeniable Yiddish quality permeates *Mazel
and Schlimazel: or The Milk of a Lioness*. At his
lowest moment, the young hero Tam sounds like a
Job-as-schlimiel figure:

> I once had parents, but they were unlucky. My father
> died of consumption. My mother went to the forest to
> gather mushrooms and was bitten by a poisonous snake.
> The small piece of land they left me is so full of rocks
> that I can hardly farm it. And last year there was a
> drought and a locust plague. This year I won't even
> have a harvest because I had nothing to sow.

Still, the underlying structure of the story goes beyond, or beneath, any provincial, or ethnic, motif. In a
word, the theme of *Mazel and Schlimazel* can be
described in the terms set forth by Otto Rank in *The
Myth of the Birth of the Hero*. Rank sees the essen-
tials of the hero myth as follows: noble parents, aban-
donment in a body of water or a small, confined space,
and the rescuing and rearing by low-born parents.

This precedes the hero's finding and returning to his original parents. According to Rank, these two sets of parents correspond to the real and imaginary parent couples of the fantasy. Psychologically they are identical in both infantile and neurotic fantasy life. *Mazel and Schlimazel* does not follow the paradigm of the myth of every point, but it contains no more variants than the materials Rank himself uses to extrapolate the paradigm; and there are, indeed, strong lines of similarity. Moreover, the variations of the paradigm in *Mazel and Schlimazel* support and enhance Rank's analysis of the psycho-sexual meaning of the myth. Singer's story contains these analogous Rankian motifs:

1. The young hero, Tam, has been raised by humble parents.

2. Although he has not been exposed at birth, like Oedipus or Moses, Tam may be regarded, for all intents and purposes, as an abandoned child.

3. In the evolution of the story, Tam rises in stature and fulfills the promise of nobility that the Rankian pattern outlines. Although Tam is not *literally* of noble birth in *Mazel and Schlimazel* (like the abandoned Oedipus), he nonetheless acts like the son of nobility, performs all the hero's tasks successfully, and is recognized by the king's daughter, Nesika, as possessing noble traits. Nesika says, "Many a prince could learn from him."

*Mazel and Schlimazel* differs from the Rankian paradigm in three important ways:

1. As has been mentioned already, Tam is not *literally* the king's son, though he does become his son-in-law.

2. There are not, strictly speaking, two parent-couples. With respect to the Rankian pattern, the queen is conspicuously absent.

3. There is even more of a mythic decomposition of

the ego, a splitting of the self, in Singer's story than in Rank's paradigm. As I shall argue, Mazel and Schlimazel may be taken *both* as father-surrogates and as projections of Tam's divided self. Beyond this, Kamstan, the Prime Minister, is a further reduplication of the father as Schlimazel.

These variations upon the myth can be explained by looking at Rank's psychoanalytic explanation and then seeing how Singer's fairy tale—because of its special psychological contours—requires a *more defensive structure* than the materials Rank is dealing with. Rank's analysis of the underlying structure of the myth may be put this way: the young child wished to grow up like mother or father. Later, he becomes aware of other parents. By comparison, his parents no longer seem unique and ideal. Trifling incidents may even lead the child to feel that other parents are preferable. The child's feeling that his love is not fully reciprocated seeks relief in the idea of being a stepchild, or an adopted child. Intense emotions of sexual rivalry are also involved in this connection. In other words, Rank interprets the myth in essentially pre-oedipal terms; he puts particular emphasis upon the "ideal" quality of the young child's image of the parents. This becomes especially clear when Rank asserts that the child in fantasy forsakes the real father for the idealized parent image of his earliest years. There is no question that there is a strong pre-oedipal element in *Mazel and Schlimazel*. Beyond the main lines of the story—which owes its design to the earliest phase of epigenetic development—an emphasis is put upon nurturing. The decisive task, after all, that Tam must perform in order to win Nesika's hand is "to fetch the milk of a lioness." To be sure, the milk of a lioness is required by the king, but it is required by the king *because he is ill*, because, in a sense, he is helpless, because, like a child, he needs to be taken care of. This connection between the king's need of the lioness's milk and Tam's need for life-sustaining milk is re-enforced when we remember that when Tam finally wins the princess "she wore a dazzling coronet with the diamond image of a lioness." The pre-oedipal relationship between child and mother, as it is expressed magically in the relationship between child and animal, resonates beautifully in the title story of *Zlateh the Goat*. The child and his beloved goat, Zlateh, are forced to seek refuge from a winter storm in a haystack for three days. With no other means of survival, Aaron must turn to Zlateh's milk.

> He looked at Zlateh and noticed her udders were full. He lay down next to her, placing himself so that when he milked her he could squirt the milk into his mouth. It was rich and sweet. Zlateh was not accustomed to being milked that way, but she did not resist. On the contrary, she seemed eager to reward Aaron for bringing her to a shelter whose very walls, floor, and ceiling were made of food.

A world of deprivation becomes a world of temporary plenty. This rhythm of emptiness and satiety fits not only the psychobiological realities of the early infant, but it harmonizes as well with the actuality of Singer's early life.

> All the neighbors sent *shalach-monos*—Purim gifts. From early afternoon the messengers kept coming. They brought wine, mead, oranges, cakes, and cookies. One generous man sent a tin of sardines; another, smoked salmon, a third, sweet-and-sour fish. They brought apples carefully wrapped in tissue paper, dates, figs—anything you could think of. The table was heaped with delicacies. Then came the masked mummers, with helmets on their heads and cardboard shields and swords, all covered with gold or silver paper. For me it was a

glorious day. But my parents were not pleased with this extravagance.

There is, then, a strong pre-oedipal element in *Mazel and Schlimazel,* and it is the pre-oedipal element that gives the story its basic design and makes it recognizable as another rags to riches story, another romance, a Yiddish *Prince and the Pauper*, if you will. *But there are also strong oedipal and post-oedipal elements in the story, and these elements can account for the variations that we find in Singer's story.* The most revealing aspect of the oedipal configuration of the story is Tam's slip of the tongue, or, if we wish, the control of his speech by Schlimazel. When Tam brings the milk of the lioness to the King—at the expiration of the contract between Mazel and Schlimazel in which Mazel has been allowed to control Tam's destiny for a year—he says, "Your majesty, I have brought what you sent for—the milk of a dog." The king is angered, of course, and says, "You will pay for this with your life." Can we find any unconscious determinants for this surfacing of hostility, for the return of repressed hostility? If we interpret the "milk of a lioness" as a symbolization of the mother, then Tam's giving the milk to the king is tantamount to the capitulation of the child to the father. Such submission is always accompanied with anger, and we will remember in thinking of the story as a whole, that, although Tam has been favored by the king, he also has been commanded to perform certain tasks, to submit to the king. From the king's point of view, Tam's triumph would entail giving up his daughter, and, to the extent that he has been without a wife, the relationship between the king and Nesika has the veiled quality of a marital relationship. It is not unlike, in a totally different social and emotional context, James's *The Golden Bowl.* From this vantage point, the death by hanging to which Tam is condemned, may be construed as a manifestation of castration anxiety, both in the general sense of the child's fear of reprisal and bodily injury and in the specific sense of loss of the head. This is not, by any means, the only phallic element in the story. Indeed, we will remember that Nesika has rejected one suitor, Typpish, because "his boots were foolish." And when her father asks her how can boots be foolish, she replies, "If the head is foolish, the feet are foolish." In *The Psychoanalytic Theory of Neuroses*, Otto Fenichel links foot fetishism to its symbolic equation with penis fixation.

A tripartite analogy is established between head, foot, and penis, and the ocdipal theme is emphasized.

Once we see the strong oedipal nature of the story it is easier to explain the variations upon the myth as defensive strategies. If *consciously* we know that (a) Tam is *not* the king's son, that (b) the queen is dead, and that (c) Schlimazel is responsible for Tam's slip of the tongue, then we are unlikely, at the conscious level, to feel threatened by the underlying content of the story. But defenses have a way of revealing the impulses they defend against, just as somatic symptoms often reveal underlying psychic conflict. By studying the defenses, we can learn more about the conflicts. If we pay careful attention to the figure of Schlimazel, we will see that, despite his fictive autonomy as a spirit, he shares qualities in common with Tam. We will see that there is a Schlimazel in Tam, as it were, who must be warded off through projection. Most saliently, we are told this story about Schlimazel's childhood.

"I wasn't born Schlimazel," he said. "My father was poor, but he was a good spirit. He was a water carrier in Paradise. My mother was a servant of a saint. My

> parents sent me to Reb Zeinvel's school. They wanted
> me to become a seraph or at least an angel. But I
> hated my parents because they forced me to study. To
> spite them, I joined a gang of imps. . . . Once I turned
> myself into a frog and hid in Reb Zeinvel's snuff-box.
> When he opened it to take a pinch, I jumped out and
> bit his nose."

Like Tam, Schlimazel's parents were poor. Like
Tam, as he has been discussed in this essay, Schlimazel has hostile feelings towards authority figures.
Where Tam both competes for the princess (the
mother surrogate in this story) and fears reprisal,
Schlimzel, in his physical attributes, is similarly ambivalent.

> Schlimazel limped along beside him with the help of a
> knotty-wood cane—an old man with a wan face and
> angry eyes under his busy brows. His nose was crooked
> and red from drinking. His beard was as gray as spider
> webs. He was attired in a long black coat and on his
> head sat a peaked hat.

Freud discusses the hat as male genital organ in *The
Interpretation of Dreams*, and we may regard the
limp, *in part*, as the reverse side of this self-assertion, a
correlative for the hanging-competitive dynamic of
the story. It is important to see the common identity
of Tam and Schlimazel, because it is Schlimazel who
suffers the anxiety that attends the submerged oedipal
content of the story. It is Schlimazel who "had for
ages been suffering from sleeplessness and nightmares." It is Schlimazel who longs for the "wine of
forgetfulness." Revealingly, it is only when Schlimazel
has been given the "wine of forgetfulness"—ostensibly
the triumph of good over evil, of Mazel over Schlimazel—that Tam is able to marry the princess. The "wine
of forgetfulness" signals both the need for Tam to
overcome anxiety in winning the princess and his

movement beyond Oedipus Complex from the mother as love-object to Nesika, who, despite her role as mother-surrogate, is, after all, *not* the king's wife, is not Tam's mother image. There is a real sense in which the child must forget the mother.

If recognizing the oedipal element in the tale makes it somewhat easier to understand the role of mythic decomposition, with respect to Schlimazel, one might ask why Mazel is required as a projection of Tam's good self and as a good surrogate father. This can be answered in three ways: (a) because the Schlimazel *in* Tam provokes anxiety and guilt, he must be countered by the Mazel *in* Tam, by the son's love for the father; (b) because the whole story is characterized by magical thinking, it is only natural that a "good" father should be projected along with the "punishing" father-surrogates, Schlimazel and Kamstan; and (c) because the conflict between father and son is inadmissible to the child's consciousness, at least the conflict generated by oedipal rivalry, it is necessary that the battle between the generations be waged, as it were, "outside" the child's mind and psyche. By having a set of doubles who represent the divided nature of the hero's ego and the good and bad father, the writer can, as we have seen, dramatize intra-psychic conflict indirectly (the Mazel *in* Tam against the Schlimazel *in* Tam). By having a set of doubles who represent both the divided nature of the hero's ego and the good and bad father, the writer can dramatize *also*—if he is ingenious, as Singer is—the conflict between father and son: i.e., although Mazel is in some sense Tam's good father, he is also *younger* than Schlimazel. Seen from this perspective, the conflict between Mazel and Schlimazel is thus a reduplication of the latent conflict between Tam and the king. In battling against Schlimazel, Mazel—either as the Mazel *in* Tam or as

Tam disguised as the young, "good" father—becomes something other than wholly "good." Though Mazel is consciously overcoming the "evil" Schlimazel, he expresses less consciously the son's rage against the father. If Mazel symbolizes *Eros*, he also embodies *Thanatos*. Equally, if Schlimazel symbolizes *Thanatos*, he also embodies *Eros*. Rage against the father cannot be separated from love for the mother and the rage against the father is inhibited by love of the father. *You can't, as it were, have your Mazel without Schlimazel*. A realistic view of father and son relationships cannot endow either the son or the father with only love *or* hate.

A consideration of the variations of the Rankian paradigm must also take into account Kamstan's role in the story. He is, as the king's "evil" Prime Minister, the naturalistic equivalent of Schlimazel, the counterbalance to the "good" king, though we have seen that, at a deeper level, the king isn't as good as we may first believe. At both the naturalistic and supernatural levels, there is an authorial effort in *Mazel and Schlimazel* to protect the king, to disguise his anger through substitution and projection. The repression of the child's anger requires the denial of any possible threat that the father may pose.

If we, imaginatively, set Tam against the sanctified father of *In My Father's Court* and God the Father of that same court, it will not seem surprising that the implied father-son conflict in *Mazel and Schlimazel* can be expressed only in the context of an elaborate defensive structure. Theoretically, we would expect that longing for the mother would be repressed equally, but Singer seems, in this particular story, to have unconsciously portrayed the mother, in part at least, at an earlier stage of the child's development; and the history of literature suggests that the loss of the nurturing mother can gain access to consciousness more readily than can an imagined loss from the oedipal period. If one thinks, as example, of *Jane Eyre* and *Sons and Lovers*, it becomes clear that, ironically, the most primitive kind of loss, the loss of the nurturing parents, can be expressed more openly than the loss of the mother to the father. If we think of those two works again, it is also clear that the lost mother of the oedipal conflict is represented in the divided figures of Miriam and Clara and that the antagonistic father is represented in the figure of Baxter Dawes: i.e., it would seem that splitting of love-objects is an especially effective defense mechanism for the handling of oedipal conflict.

If we turn back to *In My Father's Court* in another context, the myth of the birth of the hero, it becomes equally unsurprising that the Rankian pattern should appear in *Mazel and Schlimazel*. Throughout *In My Father's Court*, there are previsions of the hero's life. Singer says, "I, too, was descended from the priestly line." In the Chapter, "The Washerwoman," he remembers that the old lady who had taken in their wash thought he "looked like Jesus." He recalls that his father had told the children that "all Jews are the children of a great King." He wonders about his origins: "Perhaps, I too had been abandoned as an infant?" At one point, he thinks of himself in storybook terms: "I am alone in the world—a lost prince, just like in the storybooks. . . . The dreamer cometh. . . . Let us slay him and cast him in some pit. . . . Let us sell him to the Ishmaelites."

These fragments suggest that pan-cultural fantasies are irrepressible, that an imaginative child, no matter how isolated, will find in himself a larger world, will universalize his experience. At the same time, the very real movement out to a larger world, including the discovery of world literature, enhances this process of universalization. When we think of *In My Father's Court* in the light of *The Myth of the Birth of the Hero*, there is a specific sense in which the limited sphere of the Talmudic home supports the world-myth. The world that Singer knew growing up was a divided one: Jew and gentile, Satan and God, empirical mother and mystical father, experienced brother and virginal hero. Such bifurcations of sensibility and value lead easily into the class division of the myth, low and high born, and into the double parentage that structures this class division. Perhaps, this is another way of saying that the categories and circumscriptions of the young Singer's world are not inimical to the magical thought processes and defensive strategies of *Mazel and Schlimazel*. This point could be supported by seeing the relationship between the autonomous character of the legal *word* in the autobiography and the magical power of the symbol, the chalk, in *The Fearsome Inn*.

Perhaps it is appropriate, finally, to think of Freud's work in general and *The Interpretation of Dreams* in particular. The way *in*, the journey towards self-knowledge, became the way *out*; the exploration of unintelligible dreams opened upon the broad plain of universal experience. In exile, the Jew has dreamed traditionally of the brotherhood of man.

# Gimpel and the Archetype of the Wise Fool

PAUL N. SIEGEL

"Gimpel the Fool," perhaps the most widely acclaimed work of Isaac Bashevis Singer, has its roots deep in the soil of Yiddish literature. It is concerned with two of what Irving Howe and Eliezer Greenberg tell us, in their *Treasury of Yiddish Stories,* are "the great themes of Yiddish literature," "the virtue of powerlessness" and "the sanctity of the insulted and the injured," and has as its anti-hero the "wise or sainted fool" who is an "extreme variation" of "the central figure of Yiddish literature," "*dos kleine menschele,* the little man." The wise or sainted fool is, however, not merely a recurring character in Yiddish fiction; he is a centuries-old archetypal figure of western literature. The manner in which Singer handles this archetypal figure, making use of the ideas associated with it, but in his own distinctive way, makes "Gimpel the Fool" the masterpiece of irony that it is.

The idiot was regarded in the Middle Ages and in the Renaissance as being under the special protection of God. He was also often regarded as an "innocent" or a "natural," a child of nature who lived without thought of the past or the future and was consequently happier than the supposedly wise man. The court jester was either a feeble-minded person or a lunatic who evoked amusement by his inaneness or his antics. He might also be someone who pretended to be a fool and used his assumed folly as a license for his wit.

Shakespeare's Feste and Touchstone are jesters of the second kind, "fools" who, as Viola says of Feste (*Twelfth Night*, III, i, 61), are "wise enough to play the fool." Feste demonstrates the foolishness of Olivia in her exaggerated mourning for her brother, and Touchstone satirizes the foolish artificialities of the court. Each finds the world to be made up of fools, of whom it might be said (in the words of Touchstone (*As You Like It*, V, i, 30–31), "The fool doth think he is wise, but the wise man knows himself to be a fool."

Lear's fool is mentally unbalanced but shrewdly perceptive, crack-brained but sharp-witted. He knows the ways of the world and exposes the folly of Lear in seeking to give up power but to retain the pomp of power. Paradoxically, however, while mocking Kent for foolishly following someone who has given up his power, he himself remains faithful to Lear. In doing so, he is following a higher wisdom than worldly wisdom. This is the wisdom of St. Paul, who warned that those whom the world regarded as wise must become fools in the eyes of the world if they were to become genuinely wise. They must become as the little children of whom Christ spoke. The "innocent" or "natural" fool might act on such wisdom without thought or utter Christlike truths without realizing their significance.

The heydey of the wise fool was in Renaissance literature. However, the idea was continued in different forms in Coleridge's crazed mariner, the "graybeard loon" who has learned the secret of the love of living things; in Melville's young black boy Pip, who on being alone, like the ancient mariner, in the vast immensity of the ocean, has been rendered idiotic but has seen in its "wondrous depths" the "hoarded heaps" of "the miser-merman, Wisdom"; in Dostoevsky's saintly Prince Myshkin, reviled as an "idiot," who experiences a vision of light at the beginning of his epileptic fits.

Gimpel differs from the other representatives of the archetype, the Yiddish ones as well as the others, in that he is the expression of his creator's own idiosyncratic mixture of faith and skepticism. It is this mixture which, as we shall see in analyzing the story, is the source of its pervasive irony. Singer stated in a *Commentary* interview on November, 1963 that it would be foolish to believe the purveyors of fantasies about psychic phenomena—just as it was foolish of Gimpel to believe the fantastic lies he was told—yet the universe *is* mysterious, and there is something of truth after all in these fantasies, at least a revelation concerning the depths of the human psyche from which these fantasies emerged and perhaps something more as well. The need to continue to search for the truth, the realization that this search cannot result in the attainment of the truth, the need to choose belief, the realization that, intellectually speaking, such a choice cannot be defended against the unbeliever—all of this lies behind "Gimpel the Fool."

In many ways the work dealing with the idea of the wise fool that is closest in spirit to "Gimpel the Fool" is Erasmus's *The Praise of Folly*. Although Erasmus accepted Christianity as divinely revealed, he was capable of writing, "I like assertions so little that I would easily take sides with the skeptics wherever it is allowed by the inviolable authority of Holy Scripture and the decrees of the Church." Socrates, the man who was so wise because he knew how little he knew, he regarded as a saint equal to St. Paul. He attended the same school of the Brethren of the Common Life and imbibed there the same philosophy of a simple Christianity devoid of scholastic subtleties as did Nicholas of Cusa, who in his *Of Learned Ignorance*

maintained that all human knowledge is only speculation and that wisdom consists of the recognition of
man's ignorance and the apprehension of God
through intuition. The expression of a fusion of skepticism and faith resembling that which underlies
"Gimpel the Fool." Erasmus's *The Praise of Folly* is
pervaded by a similar complex ironic ambiguity. It
will be interesting and illuminating, as we proceed in
our discussion of Singer's story, to observe the similari-
ties between these two works.

Gimpel is the butt of his village because of his
credulity. But is he the fool that the village takes him
to be? Telling his story himself, he affirms his own
folly in his very first words: "I am Gimpel the fool."
In the very next breath, however, he takes it back: "I
don't think myself a fool. On the contrary. But that's
what folks call me." As he relates the story of his life,
this denial of his foolishness seems to be the pitiful
defense of his intellect by an evidently weak-witted
person who at times tacitly admits that he is a fool,
but a steadily deepening ambiguity plays about his
narrative. This ambiguity, present from the beginning,
is indicated in the title and the opening sentence of
the Yiddish, where the epithet used is "*chochem*" or
"sage," which often has the ironic meaning of "fool,"
the meaning in which the villagers and Gimpel's wife
use it.

Singer's device of having Gimpel act as the narrator
is similar to Erasmus's device of having the allegorical
figure of Folly deliver a mock encomium of folly. Are
we to take what she has to say seriously? Her oration is
in the form of a mock encomium, that is, it is an
ironic praising of folly which, it would seem, should
be read as the opposite, as a censuring of folly. But
then, it is delivered by Folly herself. If Folly censures
folly, then it would seem as if Wisdom should praise

it. But if Wisdom praises folly and Folly censures it, how are we to know which is Wisdom and which is Folly? We are lost in a labyrinth of irony similar to that which we shall find in "Gimpel the Fool."

Gimpel, looking back upon his childhood, seeks to justify the way in which he would allow himself to be taken in. He once played hookey because he had been told that the rabbi's wife had been brought to childbed. But how was he to know that he was being lied to: he hadn't paid any attention to whether her belly was big or not. So too, when he took a detour because he heard a dog barking, how was he to know that it was a mischievous rogue imitating a dog? These excuses of Gimpel sound plausible enough, the first as well as the second. After all, we don't expect a child to note the advance of pregnancy. Each birth is unexpected and comes as a kind of miracle that may happen to any woman.

But as Gimpel continues to explain that he was not really a fool, we see that he was indeed stupidly credulous, accepting the most fantastic stories which all the villagers conspired together to make him believe. Working as an apprentice in the bakery after he left school, he was subjected to a never ending flow of accounts of alleged wonders, each more silly than the other. Whereas before it was the rabbi's wife who was said to have given birth, now the rabbi was said to have given birth to a calf in the seventh month. But, as outrageously ridiculous as the stories are, there is still some uncertainty about how utterly a fool Gimpel is. He had to believe, he tells us, or else people got angry, exclaiming, "You want to call everyone a liar?" His belief, then, was in part the wise acquiescence of the butt who must play his role, knowing that otherwise he will never be free of his wiseacre tormentors.

Yet it was not merely a pretended belief. For always

there would come the thought: maybe it is, after all, true? When he was told that the Messiah had come and that his parents had risen from the grave, he knew very well, he informs us, that nothing of the sort had occurred, but nevertheless he went out. "Maybe something had happened. What did I stand to lose by looking?" The jeering he got on that occasion made him resolve to believe nothing more, but he could not stick to this resolution, his poor wits being no match for those of the villagers, who confused him with their argumentation.

Moreover, he came to believe not merely because he was talked into it but also because he wanted to believe. When he was derisively matched with the village prostitute, he knew very well what she was, that her limp was not, as alleged, a coy affectation and that her supposed little brother was actually her bastard child. But, after having been pushed into marriage with her by the entire village, he grew to love her and the uncertain belief in her virtue to which he had been persuaded became a determinedly held belief against all the evidence.

At this point in his narrative Gimpel, the husband of the sharp-tongued Elka, becomes both a henpecked husband and a cuckold, the two figures who have been objects of mirth through the centuries and have often as here been combined in the same person. With comic repetition each time the truth is revealed to him he is talked out of it or talks himself out of it. Elka bears a child seventeen weeks after the wedding, but after a period of pain he allows himself, having grown to love the child, to believe that it is his. She bears another child after a separation of more than nine months. The village laughs, but Gimpel accepts it as his. He finds Elka in bed with another man, but after a period of painful separation persuades himself

to accept her story that it was an illusion. On returning home unexpectedly after the separation, he finds
her in bed with his apprentice, but again he permits
himself to be persuaded that what he saw was an
illusion, this time allowing himself to be overwhelmed
by her torrent of abuse and giving up all doubt the
following morning when the apprentice replies to his
questioning with amazed denials.

His credulity has no limits. Repetition seems to
make it easier for him to believe rather than the
reverse. We should laugh at this spectacle of the fool
continuing in his folly, but we do not, for we have
come to wonder if Gimpel, undoubted fool that he
has proven himself to be, is not in reality superior to
his deceivers. Early in his torments the rabbi had
advised him, "It is written, better to be a fool all your
days than for one hour to be evil. You are not a fool.
They are the fools. For he who causes his neighbor to
feel shame loses Paradise himself." The paradox is
that Gimpel, born to be a fool all of his days, is not a
fool. It is the smart-aleck villagers, devoting their time
to playing games upon him, who are fools.

"A whole town can't go altogether crazy," reflects
Gimpel, when all of his neighbors join in urging him
to marry Elka. But the poor fool is quite wrong. A
whole town can be united in its wrongheaded lunatic
folly. Folly, as Erasmus's Folly saw, is to be found
everywhere in the world. The microcosmic world of
Singer's village of fools is reminiscent of the medieval
vision of humanity as constituting a ship of fools
embarked on the voyage of life and of the Renaissance
vision of life as a drama witnessed by God in which
the characters play their parts on "this great stage of
fools," to use the words uttered by Lear (IV, vi, 187)
when his mind is illuminated in his madness.

The paradox of Gimpel the fool being less foolish

than his neighbors does not stop there. The rabbi himself, revered though he is and consulted by every one as a sage, has his own kind of foolishness, the foolishness of the aridly Talmudic scholar who, learned though he is, may be less wise than the man who acts upon natural feeling. It is a foolishness similar to that of the scholastic philosophers, to whose intellectual sterility Erasmus's Folly counterposed the simplicity of the "babes and sucklings, that is to say, Fools," to whom Christ revealed "the Mystery of Salvation." When Gimpel goes to consult the rabbi after having found Elka with a lover, the rabbi advises that he must not stay under the same roof with her, and when Gimpel, longing for Elka and the child, convinces himself that it was an hallucination, the rabbi will not permit Gimpel to rejoin her until the case has been reconsidered. He permits Gimpel, however, to send his wife money and bread during this period. And so for nine long months poor Gimpel, who asks for nothing more than to be with his wife and child, supports them without seeing them until an obscure reference in Maimonides can be found that will release him from his unhappiness. Who, it may be asked, is the greater fool, the rabbi or Gimpel?

If the rabbi will permit Gimpel to return to Elka only after Gimpel has stated his conviction that he had suffered from an hallucination, Gimpel himself excuses Elka even if a man were actually there, saying to himself that women are easily deceived. He would have gone back to her even if he had not convinced himself that he had been mistaken. In fact, we may say that the conviction to which he comes, although sincere, is also a means by which Gimpel the "*chochem*" circumvents the rigid prescription of the revered sage.

Just as he made a vow before not to believe anything that he was told, a vow which he was unable to keep, so he now makes a vow to believe whatever he is told. "What's the good of *not* believing? Today it's your wife you don't believe; tomorrow it's God Himself you won't take stock in." It is undoubtedly laughable that Gimpel makes faith in the sluttish Elka equivalent to faith in the divine scheme of things. Yet Singer himself, during the *Commentary* interview in November, 1963, in expounding the philosophy of "as if," the doctrine that all of us must lead our lives in accordance with certain assumptions, such as the assumption that we will go on living, even if these assumptions go contrary to the existing evidence, makes use of faith in one's wife as an illustration.

So too Erasmus's Folly makes delusion in marriage representative of the delusions by which all of us must live if society and human life are to continue. Such delusions, a part of life, are, she says, necessary and natural. They are in Singer's words the "as if" by which life is maintained. Gimpel's equating of faith in Elka with faith in the divine scheme of things may thus be seen as an expression of the wisdom of simple, natural folk who accept the things of this world without thought.

Gimpel's belief in Elka despite the evidence of his own senses springs from his love for her. Where love is great, there must be faith. But Gimpel's love is not confined to Elka. It extends to all living things. This is why his faith in her is related to his faith in the divine order. Faith, hope, and charity—Gimpel has the qualities, the tenderness and the forgiveness, of the fool in Christ. In his childhood, he states, he was no weakling: if he were to slap any one, the other would see all the way to Cracow, but he wasn't a slugger by nature and accepted without retaliation his playmates' jokes on him. "I wanted to be angry," he says, telling of his longing for Elka and the child after he discovered her deception of him, "but that's my misfortune exactly, I don't have it in me to be really angry." And so throughout his life he continues to bear his burdens without anger, telling himself philosophically, "What's one to do? Shoulders are from God, and burdens too."

It is his lovingness, indeed, which makes it possible for him to continue to be deceived. The first time that he comes upon Elka in bed with a man the thought comes to him that if he makes an uproar he will awake the child, and so he steals away without doing anything and is able to persuade himself later that it was an hallucination. The second time, when he catches Elka sleeping with the apprentice, she awakes and quickly tells him to go look at the nannygoat, which she says has been ill. Gimpel, who has a "nearly human feeling" for the nannygoat, goes to examine it, and when he returns the apprentice is gone. If Elka and the apprentice, however, reply to Gimpel's tenderness and kindliness with deceit, the simple things of nature, the infant and the nannygoat, "a good little creature," respond affectionately to him. They are, as Erasmus's Folly said of the little children and the guileless animals of whom Christ spoke—the sheep, Christ's term for the souls destined to eternal life, Folly pointed out, is the most foolish animal of all— creatures "living only by the dictates of Nature and without either craft or care."

Before Elka dies, she confesses to Gimpel that she has deceived him all of their married life. The Spirit of Evil comes to Gimpel as he is sleeping and, telling him that God and the judgment in the world to come are fables, persuades him to revenge himself against the deceitful world by urinating in the dough so that the "*chachomim*," the sages of the village, may be fooled into eating filth. When Gimpel had queried Elka about the apprentice, she had screamed, "An evil spirit has taken root in you and dazzles your sight," and he had thought to himself, "All that's needed now is that people should accuse me of raising spooks and dybbuks. . . . No one will touch bread of my baking." Now his resentful thoughts have indeed conjured up an evil spirit which momentarily blinds him and causes him to bake bread which should not be touched. (Indeed, Singer in the *Commentary* interview mentioned earlier stated that he believes in demons both substantively as literally existing powers and symbolically as representing human behavior.)

After he has baked the unclean bread, however, and lies dozing by the oven, Elka appears in a dream. She calls him *"chochem"*—ironically wise man and fool—for believing that because she was false everything else is a lie. She had in reality never deceived anyone but herself, and now she is paying for it in the other world. In her screams in child-labor she had anticipated her death-bed confession, calling, "Gimpel, I'm going. Forgive me," but when she had recovered she did not mend her ways. Now it is too late.

The "as if" that Elka is faithful by which Gimpel had lived is now seen by him to give way, after it has sunk under him, to other "as if's." He buries the bread in the ground, divides his wealth among the children —he had earlier casually mentioned in his unworldly way that he had forgotten to say that he had come to be rich—and goes into the world. Before he had regarded his village as the world. Now he finds out that the world has much more in it than he knew. He grows old and gray in his wanderings. He hears many fantastic tales, but the longer he lives the more he comes to realize that there are no lies. Everything, no matter how fantastic, comes to pass sooner or later.

The something that was supposed to have happened that he hears and regards as impossible actually happens at a later time. Or even, he says in a sentence omitted in the Bellow translation, a sentence reminiscent of Singer's comment on the magazines devoted to psychic phenomena, if a story is quite imagined, it also has a significance: why does one person dream up one thing and another person an entirely different thing?

Gimpel thus becomes a representative of that other variant of *dos kleine menschele* in Yiddish fiction, "the ecstatic wanderer, hopeless in this world because so profoundly committed to the other," as Greenberg and Howe have put it. He also becomes reminiscent of the Wandering Jew, who according to the legend transmitted through the centuries was punished for having spat into the face of Christ by being deprived of the power to die. Cursed with unwanted life, imbued with the esoteric knowledge he has acquired through having lived through many civilizations, he is generally an evil figure, but he is also sometimes represented as Christ-like in the sustained agony through which he pays for his sin. Longing to join Elka in death, weary from the years of his wandering, Gimpel is transformed by the realization that has come to him from his varied experiences that "the world is entirely an imaginary world," becoming a personification of the ecstatic wisdom that is attained through the agony of suffering.

Yet the wisdom he has attained is the same that he had when, "like a golem," he "believed everyone," reasoning to himself, "Everything is possible, as it is written in the Wisdom of the Fathers, I've forgotten just how." What had seemed to be one of a number of excuses offered by a fool for his gullibility turns out to be indeed wisdom. The outrageously outlandish stories about miraculous births he had accepted really attested to his perception of the miracle of life. The hallucinations which he told himself he had had really attested to his perception that the world is a dream.

But now he who had listened to stories of marvels is the one who tells them: "Going from place to place, eating at strange tables, it often happens that I spin yarns—improbable things that could never have happened—about devils, magicians, windmills, and the like." Sometimes the children who chase after him tell him the particular story they wish to hear, and he satisfies them with a recital of that tale. For Gimpel, it is implied, has come to understand that each one of us has his own favorite fiction to which he is addicted, his own delusion to which he needs to remain faithful. But a sharp youngster tells him that it is really always the same story that he tells. For all of our delusions derive from the dream that is life in this world. The tales which the aged wanderer relates deal with the folk superstitions to which there have been so many references in "Gimpel the Fool"—the windmills, however, seem to be a reminiscence of the illusions of that glorious madman, Don Quixote—but these superstitions, silly as they are, are glimpses of the truth shadowed forth in the dream of life: "No doubt the world is entirely an imaginary world, but it is only once removed from the true world."

Dreams themselves are visions of a higher reality. The moment Gimpel closes his eyes he sees Elka standing over the steaming washtub as he had first seen her, but it is an Elka transfigured, her face shining, her eyes radiant, her words consoling, her talk of strange things which he forgets the instant he awakes. He does, however, remember her promise that they will be reunited in a future time.

Yet Gimpel's ecstatic vision is not without its ambiguity. It is similar in this to the conclusion of *The Praise of Folly*. Folly relates how holy men through their meditations attain a brief glimpse of heavenly bliss. When they come to themselves, they do not know whether they were asleep or awake and do not remember what they experienced except that they were rapturously happy. "And therefore they are sorry they are come to themselves again, and desire nothing more than this kind of madness, to be perpetually mad. And this is a small taste of that future happiness." But Folly does not conclude with this description of the ecstatic vision of the saints. She apologizes for her boldness in dealing with such matters but reminds us of the proverb "Sometimes a fool may speak a word in season." Of course, she adds, she is a woman, and the reader may choose not to apply the proverb to women. Moreover, she does not remember what she has said, "having foolishly bolted out such a hodge podge of words," and she advises the reader not to remember them either. It is up to the individual reader, therefore, whether he is to regard the vision of the saints as mere lunacy, whether he is to regard Folly's assurance that it is a taste of future happiness as the words of wisdom which may come from the lips of a fool and whether he is to regard the advice to forget what he has heard as the advice of Folly.

So with Gimpel the Fool. Can we believe in the transformed Elka? Is the Elka who, suffering the pangs of labor, cried out for forgiveness only to relapse into a life of deception capable of such a transformation? Must not reunion with her after the separation of death be similar to the disillusioning reunion with her after the previous separation? Is Gimpel's vision really a foolish dream?

He awakes to taste the salt of the tears Elka had shed over him as she stroked and kissed him. But on previous occasions he had wept himself asleep or had awakened crying. Is this what he is left with now—his own tears? He awaits death as entrance to the true world: "Whatever may be there, it will be real, without complication, without ridicule, without deception. God be praised: there even Gimpel cannot be deceived." But the first time he had found Elka in bed with a man he had told himself, "Enough of being a donkey. Gimpel isn't going to be a sucker all his life. There's a limit even to the foolishness of a fool like Gimpel," yet he had gone on permitting himself to be duped. Even the world of marvels he discovers as a wanderer may be, it is hinted, merely additional evidence of his credulity. "Often I heard tales of which I said, 'Now this is a thing that cannot happen.' But before a year had elapsed I heard that it had actually come to pass somewhere." He *heard* that it had come to pass *somewhere*: he had not himself witnessed it, therefore, but accepted on trust what it was told him had happened elsewhere. Is Gimpel's foolishness, then, really limitless, and is his final assurance that he will attain the world of reality after death either another self-deception or the continuation of an endless deception practiced upon him by malevolent Higher Powers? Will death, instead of blissful certainty, bring him either nothingness or another world of dreams and deception?

The reader is left with this teasing ambiguity, but the intensity of Gimpel's vision is such that it is consigned to the back of his mind. "I choose to believe," said Singer. It is also the choice of Gimpel, not an intellectual choice but one springing from his innermost need. If Singer makes the same choice, he is still able to look upon Gimpel with the detachment of the doubter. We need not share Singer's philosophy to be moved by the compassion mixed with irony with which he regards Gimpel, the fool who has become representative of poor, bewildered, suffering humanity.

# Index

175